FALLING G
STAIR UP
S

First published in Australia by Shore Drift,
an imprint of Harbour Publishing House, 2014

Second edition published by Fifty Days Press,
Sydney, NSW, Australia. 2020

Text copyright © Chrissy Guinery, 2020
www.chrissyguinery.com
chrissyguinery@gmail.com
@chrissyguinery

ISBN 978 0-6481992-1-2

Cataloguing-in-publication data available from
the National Library of Australia.

Printing SOS Print + Media

COVER DESIGN

Front cover photo by Jordan Innes
Back cover artwork by Mace Innes

FOLLOW THE AUTHOR

www.chrissyguinery.com

FALLING UP STAIRS

by Chrissy Guinery

Dedicated to the one who forced me into it... in the kindest possible way
And to my very first publisher and wonderful friend Garry Evans-
your memory lives on in our hearts

and

to the arrows in granny's quiver
Ella, Mia, Willow, Chili, Hayz, Oaky, Cove, Harper, London, Lennox,
Peaches, Hopps, Junee, River and the many more to come...

I'm Me

Do you see me for me?
Am I who I'm meant to be?
When I try to take a breath – I just drown in happiness
'cause I'm proud of being me
You should be proud of being you
'cause no-one's the same
You're the only you

(Myman Benny © 3.1.2000)

CONTENTS

CHAPTER ONE
drifting

'I've been falling down stairs all afternoon!' These were the excited words our youngest son blurted out when I answered his call to my mobile. The previous week it had been, 'I have been getting hit by cars for two hours!' Always excited, always filled with enthusiasm and wonder. As a mother, these are not usually the first words you want to hear when you answer your man-child's phone-calls. But, in the case of this son, I am as thrilled about it as he is.

From when he was very young he showed tendencies to leading a life on the edge, not quite satisfied with the normal or mundane. I remember when he was about seven-years-old, and he helped his dad build a skate-ramp to his own specifications, for him to practice skateboarding skills. The day he mastered tricks off that ramp, his next words were, 'Imagine the tricks I could do if we build a bigger ramp!' Barely basking in the glory of one feat accomplished, he would be challenging himself to rise to another.

He is the son many of our friends tend to cringe about whenever we reminisce about the old days. I'll give you just one of the reasons why. During his teens, we were renting a two storey house with a balcony off the back. He would take great delight in waiting until our guests were seated contentedly nibbling crackers and cheese and sipping hot cuppas, casually enjoying the afternoon sunshine, and he would choose his perfect moment to rush through the house, out through the double-doors from the dining room, run zooming past the unsuspecting party of relaxing adults, and leap over the balcony rail performing a double flip down onto the grassy lawn two storeys below. This, let me assure you, can cause an aneurysm – and I mean in the unsuspecting adults, not the crazy kid flipping off the balcony!

Despite the repeated hospital trips and concussions and broken bones, I am really thrilled about the man of vision he is. He doesn't quit, and won't give up when the going gets tough. He just gets up again and has another go. He has conquered more fear than I've even experienced. Nothing fazes him as he leaps from tall buildings. This reminds me, he still carries the scars from the first tall building he leapt off. At age nine, Mr No-Fear thought it would be a terrific stunt to skateboard off the garage roof. Had there not been a wooden paling fence in the way, it would have been a sensational fait accompli. Remember that old television series Get Smart where Secret Agent 86, aka Maxwell Smart, would declare at least once during each half-hour episode 'Missed it by that much'? Yeah, that would describe my youngest son's agonising descent as the wooden fence removed all the skin along his spine, from his shoulders down to the top of his bum. He was a real mess. But he was, and is, 'a tuff little bugger', and quitting has never been on his agenda.

At the time I began writing this, he was in the final stages of training at a stunt school, being made ready to be a professional stuntman. Before I finished this book, it became his reality. My husband and I are thrilled he is a professional stunt man. He knew what he wanted to do, and, despite being brought up in a small Aussie country town by parents without much income or influence, he achieved his dreams. He didn't notice any of the impossibilities. He never listened when people (and there were many) attempted to discourage him with 'what ifs' and 'you can't do that'. He had a dream, believed it, sowed into it, worked toward it and achieved it. He is literally now LIVING THE DREAM as they say (whoever 'they' are).

* * *

And I can officially confess, so am I. Oh, not a stuntman, but living MY dream. For want of a better place to begin, I'll tell you about my husband and I having a brilliant vision that we put together fully, about ten years back. We'd been working on it for many, many years, but it eventually came together very neatly and was a large part of the inspiration behind us launching out on our bold adventure, about five years ago. After selling or giving-away what little we owned, we took off to travel Australia in our little LiteAce van (literally not much more than a bed on wheels) affectionately known as Buzz - a cute little technicolour original, covered in designs and paintings, compliments of our friends and family.

And what an amazing, inspiring vision for our lives it is! We carried the vision with passion for years... and then, almost without noticing, we lost it. We drifted away and it faded into the background and we forgot our vision. Now that we have resurrected it, it seems impossible for us to comprehend. That is totally unreal! Years and years of work to perfect a vision, carrying it in our hearts til our very lives pulsated with the joy of it, and then, one day, while our backs were turned, we'd let it fade out of our consciousness and slip through our fingers like grains of sand. How the hell did that happen? And to visionary people like US!

We share the same vision, but let me tell you, we are very different people. For instance, I love the exciting and grand. I enjoy pushing boundaries and living life on the edge (hmmm maybe that's where our youngest son gets it from). I'm one of those sanguine, extrovert, evangelist, enthusiasts who expects my glass to be bubbling over, not just half full. And if it's going to be bubbling over, let's have it filled with something scrumptious! *Everything* is BIG for me. On the other hand, my husband, a very strong man, is also a gentle person. He likes quiet times of contemplation and lots of alone-time. We are a match made in heaven, ha-ha! My over-zealous enthusiasm to suck the life-juice out of every moment of every day exhausts my methodical melancholic, 'let's think this through before we blah blah blah' partner-for-life. Yet, together, we make a dynamic team and have created a sensational family.

When our five little darlings were youngsters and they passed wind (which is an absolutely hilarious event to every child, every time), they named it after an acquaintance of ours. For real! There was no prompting from us. Truth be told, we didn't even know about this conspiracy between them until years later. This man that our children named their flatulence after turned out to have some very serious problems that didn't come to light until many years later, so the kids were on the money. It was like they knew, instinctively, there was something not right about him, and that was their way of dealing with it. Still to this day popping-off makes me smile as I think of my children's genius. Family life is such a buzz. Hubby and I are holidaying at my mum's home, the one I grew up in, as I'm writing this, and she is a typical mum, with photos galore hung all over the place and sitting on sideboards, with smiling faces and twinkling eyes from many eras stalking you from every room. Looking at the photos always makes us laugh. I mean, at the time they were taken I am sure everyone thought we were pretty cool, suave cats; obviously. But looking back is always a hoot – and our kids literally moan at what we made them wear and the hairdos they had to endure. It can put you in a nostalgic mood though, surrounded by memorabilia from all directions of your bloodline.

Time flies by so quickly. I almost feel like a dinosaur. Me and my hubby are looking back at these photos and wondering how on earth we survived. All five children were born within the same decade we were married in, so forgive me for my ignorance on any world events during this ten year period (I barely had time to look outside our backdoor into our own backyard, let alone our nation). When I consider the energy and effort it took to raise them, it almost feels like martyrdom. I fear today's modern family looks very different to ours. Things are changing so rapidly, it's like the new family seems more about a house, car and pets than it is children. I hope I don't seem too strange a creature; one who chose staying home and going without to nurture the offspring we created.

The joy my healthy, crazy, loving, chaotic family bring is boundless. I love getting the gang together these days. Wow, chaos reigns. Centre of the long, extended dining table in my eldest daughter's home, I observe the crazy antics of our ever-expanding family. There are 17 of us now. Four of our five children have married, one is engaged, two are with-child, and three have children of their own; so mealtimes are glorious experiences if you can survive the deafening din. It is a kind of romantic chaos, and as I look about me over the table amidst the sounds of chatter and laughter and friendly teasing and the swapping of stories, I believe I am to be envied. It feels so great. To love and be loved, and see the circle of love swirling round and round the table, expressed in family 'in' jokes, the stealing of food off one another's plates, kiddies scampering from knee to knee of the adults in order to glean the best bits off dinner plates while the big people aren't looking. Family meals without such frivolity can have no soul; we probably couldn't digest our food without the madness. It has become the 'norm', even though, to this changing modern world, it is probably totally 'ab'normal.

I often find myself laying in bed in Buzz (that's the technicolour van), exhausted, after another wild weekend, relishing the fact that I had once again enjoyed one of life's most rewarding experiences of blood and in-laws and little girls and a bouncing baby boy mixed together with dinners and breakfasts, and games and playgrounds – all combined to make a rich cocktail of family laughter, bonding, sharing and doing life together. I feel infinitely blessed, as though through weekends like that, I receive a tiny glimpse into heaven.

Even though my children and grandchildren are growing up all around me, I'm personally stuck in a time-warp. I keep thinking I'm still in my 40s. And I'm not! It isn't because I'm young-looking, because I'm not that either. It isn't exactly that I'm so super-fit, because I'm not that neither. It's just my mind can't get past my 40s. I've seen those older women, dressed like teens, those ones my mum clicks her tongue in disgust about and describes as 'mutton dressed as lamb', as though it's a terrible, terrible thing. They don't have perms in their hair, they don't colour their grey curls purple, they don't wear 'just below the knee' length floral dresses and have a string of pearls about their wrinkly necks. I don't set out to be one of them, but if I'm not 40 anymore, and I'm not, then there is a very strong possibility that I am one of those older muttons dressed as lamb. But is the conscious reality of age really that important? I mean really? If we are enjoying life and living peacefully and happily, can there really be any harm in fooling ourselves about numbers? Aren't numbers for mathematicians? (Or 'mathemagicians' as my eight-year-old granddaughter calls them.)

I'm content to be me. I wear wild clothes, odd dangly earrings, and enjoy short, messy hairdos. I sport a dozen mismatched bracelets on my left wrist and am quite comfortable wearing gold and silver rings on the same finger ha-ha. I love to laugh (a far cry from how I began). Are you happy with who you are, or are you continuously attempting to fit some stereotype? Is your house decorated like the magazines say it should be done, or is it fitting to your personality? Do you dress off the racks from the latest boutiques, or are you comfortable in wearing things that actually suit you and make you feel good? Allow me to encourage you to forget about numbers, age, trends and fashion – begin to just enjoy being yourself. We all have a yearning within us to be accepted for who we are; not by 'becoming' someone else. We're not meant to want to 'be' others, but to be 'loved by' others. Our potential, skills and talents are unique to *us*. And we all know an *original* is always worth more than a copy.

To be content with who we are is where real happiness begins, and that is when we're most effective in life. It took me a very long, difficult and tumultuous time to figure this out; gory details of which you will be privy to soon. Meantime, I have discovered that we are free to explore new ways to make our life fun – the play, rest *and* work – being creative and entertaining along the way. Your happy vibes will shine out upon all who see you, and the loving will continue. I know this advice to be true because I have learnt some life lessons along the way. More often than not, I learnt them the hard way.

May I introduce two themes flowing throughout this book: live on purpose and love yourself. Not in a conceited way, but simply being happy to be you. I couldn't do that for years, and it is now one of the burning passions on my heart, to see other people set free to fulfil dreams whilst enjoying themselves. I'm big on love. The alternative, that four letter 'h' word, well, I hate that! I want no part in that culture. There are enough nasty people storming the earth hating everyone and everything 'different'. The potential for meaningful relationships often lies *within* the differences. I've joined the pioneers of a new culture, one of love and acceptance, where we explore and embrace differences. A place where people are free to dream dreams and achieve them whist encouraging those around them to do the same. A planet of people who are winners, with smiles on our faces that begin in our hearts. If someone else can't make our day, let's make someone else's day!

I worked as a journalist over a ten year period, and it was during one such assignment that I gleaned some profoundly useful tips from the mayor of the city at that time, Paul Green. Within his speech not long after his election as mayor, at a ceremony for community awards, he included things like, 'Be a person that lives with purpose and conviction. Work for the highest good of another. Don't 'camp' at your failings; move on. Turn scars into stars and strengthen your positives. Resolve conflict; learn to say 'sorry'. Champion your partner, children and grandkids. Become and practice being a better lover.' And he finished quirkily with, 'Lord, make me the person my dog thinks I am!'

He expounded on these topics, but I jotted the main headers down and popped them into my quote book. I love quotes. I am the Queen of Quotes, but you'll learn that quickly enough.

Speaking of my journo days, I would need the dictionary beside me to read some of my co-workers' articles, and by the time I had figured out what the crux of the article was, I had lost interest. My vocabulary is semi-limited, because I never did get the point of using obscure words to describe something that can be done with simple, everyday, off-the-street language. On the other hand, my hubby loves big words. You know if my hubby was reading this book he would have a dictionary on hand, just to make sure I was getting words right. When he is reading any book, he has a thesaurus and a dictionary beside him and is constantly sourcing them. Who reads books like that, with a group of other books as tools beside you? (If you are one of those people, well, now's your chance – pop along and grab them.) Give me an easy-read where the author has done the work for me, any day.

Anyway, back to the plot... I was writing about our *vision*... about the pursuing of our dreams, and I mentioned us drifting away from our purpose. Drifting away from the shore can be so subtle it happens before you realise it, and when you realise it, you can be WAY out to sea!

I was holidaying in Greenpatch within a National Park on the south coast of NSW, about 25 years ago. One of my brothers and his wife and kiddies were there, and I was there with my five children. We had been playing in the safe shallow waters of the bay when my brother brought his rubber dinghy down. I told him I would 'test the waters' and jumped in and began paddling. I don't like deep water. I thoroughly enjoy the ocean when my feet can touch the bottom, and swim in it most weeks of the year, but I strongly dislike being in over my head. I can be the type that panics too easily. So it was not intentional that I got further and further away from the shore. There was a wind blowing, and with me in the dinghy it just wasn't enough weight to keep it where I wanted it. The wind increased and the wind won. Before I had realised the severity of my predicament, within what seemed like mere minutes, I had drifted into deep water and the wind was pushing me further out to sea. My family back at the shore were the size of ants and I began to panic! I rowed with all my strength but couldn't even keep the dinghy where it was, let alone stop it from being blown further from the safety zone. I really was in 'over my head' as my mind turned to sharks and drowning and that horrid feeling of absolute, complete helplessness. I prayed. I prayed with sweat pouring off my forehead and tears streaming down my face; that kind of praying.

Three men eventually came to my rescue. One was my brother, who had realised I was in trouble long before I did and had begun to swim toward me with all the strength he could muster. Another was a man who had been fishing on the edge of the point and saw the danger I was in, and another was a skindiver, in a black wetsuit who couldn't believe he had to swim so far out to get to me. All three men knew I was in serious trouble if they could not get me back to shore. So, between them, with me sitting limply within the dinghy with the oar uselessly resting upon my shaking knees, these heroic men swam and tugged and pulled and pushed me back to shore. It may seem a bizarre thing to do, but I am a sanguine and an extravert as I told you, so, while these men were busting their butts to save my life, I introduced myself and asked them their names. My brother's name is David; I didn't need him to tell me that, I have known him all my life. The fisherman's name was David. The skindivers name was, yeah, David.

As the dinghy was eventually dragged to the safety of my worried, waiting family; my brother collapsed, exhausted, onto the sand. You might not pick it up in the retelling, but it was a harrowing experience. There were spectators everywhere, as, from the moment I went beyond the safe harbour and toward the sea; we had created quite a scene. I struggled on my wobbly legs to get out of the dinghy and looked around for the other two Davids. They were gone. They had disappeared! For real. We asked after them among the crowd and nobody knew anything about them. To camp at Greenpatch you need to have registered, and there was a registration board near where I had been rescued. We went through the names and there was only one David registered. My brother.

To this day we marvel at that answered desperate prayer. Were those men angels? Who knows? They were never seen of or heard from again and not one person in that entire camp could vouch for them. They simply disappeared. How bizarre!

Just as I had drifted unawares, in that dinghy that dreadful day; my hubby and I had let our dreams and goals drift away. Or, probably more correctly, we had drifted away from pursuing our purpose.

BUT, (and you have to love that little word 'but') we were taken back to the vision for our lives and we are fervent and excited and passionate and thrilled all over again... and as we re-read our plans, we can't believe what a fantastic vision we have... for us. I mean, it's ours... it's not for anyone else, it's just for us. A custom-made vision just for me and my husband. It is something we can carry in our hearts. As we meditate on the bigger picture, we refine the smaller goals we have set down toward achieving that big picture. We can dream about it and believe for it. And we can WORK toward it. Not many of us like the word 'work'. We want everything to fall into our laps. But when we are working toward something meaningful, it regenerates our sense of purpose, fun and excitement about what is happening WITH us and IN us and helps us look forward with expectation to what is planned FOR us. And it really and truly doesn't feel like work at all. My son the stuntman can vouch for that.

I'm learning to be the best I can be. I'm no guru. In fact I'm just an ordinary gal on a mission to inspire, motivate and encourage as many people as I can before I am pushing up daisies. I hope to inspire YOU with vision, to inject some enthusiasm into YOUR dreams and to have you walking out your life with renewed purpose and an added sense of belief and wonder after journeying with me on my wild roller-coaster, *Falling Up Stairs*. Purpose and vision should BURN in our hearts. Let's generate some passion. Woohoo! We were born to fulfil our purpose, not to sit back and blend into the background of life.

Nobody really makes a conscious decision to 'just have an average life', do they? Nobody decides to have a slow, boring life that doesn't influence anyone else and never really gets us inspired. All of us are centre stage in the theatre of our life; and we want to do it well. We want to make a difference; we're out to enjoy every moment we can. We simply weren't created to be mundane. Every person is so utterly, totally different, that we're all individual freaks! (I mean that in the nicest possible way.) We're weirdos. I'm strange to you because I think and dress and speak and live differently to you, and you'll seem strange to me. Don't fall into the trap of comparing yourself with me or others, or conforming to others' expectations; just be you. That's the great thing about being created by a creative God. He didn't just make clones or manufacture a bunch of robots to fulfil a quota. Each of us is a uniquely hand-crafted individual.

'Thank you for making me so wonderfully complex! Your workmanship is marvellous – how well I know it,' says Psalm 139. David, the writer of most of the psalms in the bible, probably never imagined in his wildest dreams, that his gift of poetry would bless so many. David knocked out his thoughts on paper and formed them into poems, and they became psalms of praise not only in his day, but hundreds of years later and thousands of years later!

He was just a kid when he first started writing poetry and his words continue to change lives today. What gift do you have to offer to be used to challenge, encourage and change lives? It is worth pondering.

CHAPTER TWO
kettle's wood

As colourful as the technicolour van hubby and I travel Australia in, so is my story. With wisdom gleaned through my years as a journalist, mother, waitress, writer, wife, motivational speaker, Aussie adventurer and granny, I invite you on my journey - the story of how one woman (that would be me) has grown from a cowering loser into a conquering winner. I have written *Falling Up Stairs* as a motivational tool to help others rise and run. I want you to have an idea so wonderful that it sparks your imagination, ignites your zeal, pops your cork, and puts some zing in your step. I now have an attitude of gratitude instead of stinking thinking – and it feels so darn good! I make no apologies for writing with candour, raw emotion and passion; I don't hold back in the retelling of real-life tales. With a keen eye for the lessons buried within them, I take you through the (sometimes messy) messages I've learnt through my own feelings of self-loathing, my suicide attempt, my emotional breakdown, the sexual assault as a teen, my alcohol and drug addictions, and my marriage failure and restoration. I know my life is far-from-ordinary (now) – as is evident in my offspring; the fireman, the minister, the circus instructor, the mothers, the musicians and the stuntman – and I want you to realise your life is far from ordinary too. Yet one of the biggest lessons in gaining the freedom to be me has been in taking my focus off myself, and looking for ways to help others.

Two of my daughters (eldest and youngest) and I were stopped at a busy intersection in Canberra a couple of weekends back when a man with a squeegee and a bucket gestured toward us with a 'would you like your windscreen cleaned' kind of nod. We were so excited ('what's so exciting about that?' I'm glad you asked). It wasn't that our windscreen was that filthy, but that we had a chance to surprise someone with the unexpected. As he washed the windscreen we quickly scrounged around in our purses til one of us came up with a $20 note. Just to see the look on his face was worth twice that. The reality is that $20 isn't that much money, but when he was only expecting maybe a tenth of that, I know it made him feel pretty special (there've been times in our journey when $20 in our hand has made us feel like we were holding a nugget of pure gold). I reckon those bucket-and-squeegee-bearing guys really deserve a bonus – have you seen them standing forlornly in the stifling heat, with the sun beating down on them, cars zooming past them and an odd dollar thrown their way? Anyway this guy was over-the-moon, and suddenly far more energetic as he bounced away with a big smile on his dial. It really is a buzz to create zany ways to give someone an unexpected 'kick'; and the joy bounces right back at you.

'I can never do a kindness too soon for I never know how soon it will be too late.' Don't you love that? It is so well put, I wish I knew who to give credit for it. On our travels, hubby and I have daily unexpected treats that I like to call 'kisses from heaven' where we seem to get blessed out of the blue. These kisses from heaven are both *for* us - as we receive something; and *from* us – as we get to 'smack' one (figuratively speaking), on the lips of strangers. We undertook this crazy trip of ours for many reasons, but mostly to go and share loving vibes with others. We figured we could kill two birds with one stone; see Australia, and bless others along the way.

It isn't always easy, but we can usually find some fun in it somewhere. It may not turn out as we expected (a far cry from it mostly), but it never fails to generate a sense of wonder in us. We often feel as though we are empowered with supernatural hope and optimism. Each morning we stop, ask, look and listen (a bit like crossing the road) to pick up the vibes of where we're being led. It really is as if we just *fall* into blessings. The magic ingredient is expectation! Expectation holds great potential.

Sometimes the blessings come randomly and spontaneously, and at other times we take a while to figure out the best way to give someone's day a lift. The other night at dinner, for example, we just felt to pick up the tab for a young family dining next to us. It was a joy to see the look of shock, gratefulness and confusion on their faces, and to catch the reaction of the restaurant staff when we told them we'd like to pay for *both* bills. It's a real hoot.

During a stay with our youngest daughter - who was working as a musician down in Melbourne a few years back - we were strolling through Fitzroy

Gardens for a bit of exercise and a 'tree-fix'. It was during one of our more carefree periods when our time was our own, and each morning we'd meander through the gardens to kick-start our day. We noticed there were a number of people 'living-rough' in the Gardens, with a few finding shelter under the awning of one of the old, disused buildings. We caught the eye of a younger-looking man (many avoided all eye contact) and we smiled and said, 'Gidday'. Over the days and weeks ahead, we got to know this young Chinese man (he told us his name was Vinnie) and we began to hear a little about his life.

My heart has always gone out to the homeless, but it can be difficult to know exactly what we are meant to do to help - do we offer money, food, a blanket, or do we take them home with us? These questions often bother me, but I have come to the conclusion that doing something, however small, is better than doing nothing at all.

We noticed quite a few homeless people sleeping under trees, in parks, in shop entry-ways, etc, during our sojourn in the city, so I got my thinking cap on and took action. I went to a few shelters, churches, and care-centres, and asked about the resources that were available for the homeless. Over the course of a week, I gathered all the information I could find on places where people could safely crash-out for a night or two; where they could get free meals, food and blankets, that sort of stuff. It was encouraging (it actually blew my mind and enlarged my faith in humanity during our stay there in Melbourne) to see the kindness, compassion and sacrificial-giving of some of the business-people. I compiled all the information I had gathered from businesses, charity-organisations and hostels, and had it written on sheets of paper that I could hand-out when the situation arose - along with a few gold coins – which were generally received with sincere thanks and appreciation. It was up to them what they did with the information (and the money), and while it certainly wasn't going to 'fix' their bigger issues, I felt better that I was at least having a go.

Vinnie, our new friend living-rough in the Gardens, was one of the first people I offered the list to. He was interested in the free food and told me about some extras that I could add to my list. Apparently there was also a van that drove around and offered blankets and a hot meal a few evenings throughout the winter - an initiative of one of the local churches; and he added a few extra restaurants I hadn't heard about. One of the fascinating things about Vinnie was that he told us he had chosen to be homeless, something I wouldn't have entertained or fathomed before meeting him.

Vinnie's story was that he had had a wife and a house of their own in his home-country, but they had been violently driven out. He had lost everything... including his wife, his home, and his connection with his wider family. He had developed the mindset of, 'If I never have anything of material value, I don't have to worry about it being taken away from me'. His background led him to believe that he was safer not to have a home. We tried to encourage Vinnie to see another perspective, but at the same time, we attempted to respect his outlook. After all, we hadn't had to deal with tragedies of such magnitude, so what would we know? We couldn't comprehend the depth of his pain... we who owned our little coloured van, which may seem nothing much to affluent people, but was suddenly a flippin' lot compared to zilch! We were fed and dry and mobile and comfortable. We had one another, we had all of our beautiful children and grandchildren, and we were alive and well. You know that saying, 'But for the grace of God, there go I.'

Besides Vinnie in the Gardens, we got to know a few of the 'regulars' on the streets, and we made a point of always having some gold coins on us, in case we were asked – which was most of the time. One day Dave, a young man we had given money to a couple of times, came up to my hubby. 'Hey, Step (that's how regular and familiar we were, we knew one another by name), got any money?' As I said, we usually carried something to share, but we were pretty skint ourselves at the time, so hubby said, 'No, sorry Dave, I got nothing today, mate.' Do you know what Dave said? 'Man, you're worse off than I am, Step. Why don't ya get a job?'

Along with the comic street-regulars like Dave, hanging in the Gardens with Vinnie expanded our hearts. His woeful tale continued when he explained that not many people spoke to him. Most reacted as though he wasn't there – it really does seem easier at times. I guess we're all a little bit like that. We don't know whether to look down on the homeless, ignore them, or to sit in the street and chat with them.

It's easy to fall into the trap of seeing them as less than ourselves, or inferior in some way. Connecting with Vinnie was a humbling experience for us and it taught us a lot about respecting and accepting others. Alas, there is still no easy solution for many of the people who are disadvantaged and homeless. Sometimes all we can do, and the best we can do, is to show them the kindness and respect they deserve as fellow human beings. For us, in this situation, we did our little bit to drop some love on a stranger.

Vinnie was of Chinese origin, so one day after we had decided we were about to leave the city, my hubby, who is a great cook and a creative genius in the kitchen, spent the entire afternoon in our daughter's apartment preparing a delicious Chinese banquet of spring-rolls, dim-sims, rice and a couple of other authentic dishes. He packaged up the assortment of homemade goodies in separate dishes, complete with sauces, napkins and chopsticks and delivered it to Vinnie's 'home' in the Gardens. It was our farewell gift.

* * *

Being on the road and getting to stay in places for a month or two (or a year or two as is the case at present), opens the door to meet all sorts of people from all walks of life. We often find ourselves camped near beaches, in the bush or in reserves, and people seem to be drawn to us. Our little bed-on-wheels is very colourful (and very unpretentious), so it does catch the eye. On one such occasion we received a 'kiss from heaven' without our recognising it at first. We were sitting on our camp chairs beside Buzz (as there is 'sleeping-room only' in Buzz, most of our time is spent outdoors), alongside a river somewhere in north-eastern Victoria when a motorbike roared up beside us and a large, leather-clad young man dismounted. Shedding some of his gear, we watched as he awkwardly removed a cigarette from his top pocket with hands that were shaking, beaten and bloodied. We nodded a polite 'hello' and my hubby and I went back to reading our books and soaking up the sun.

It wasn't long before Sean, the young biker, wandered over, and without any encouragement from us, began spilling out his life story in detail. He had an ex-girlfriend who was the mother of his son, and he had just 'knocked-up' his current girlfriend, but wasn't sure he wanted to be with her. Besides not feeling any deep connection with either woman or his child, he had recently lost his job and had taken to punching people and other things to relieve his frustrations. Sean poured out his heart to us, searching through his mess for some clarity and answers as he tried to make sense of his situation.

We sat there for almost two hours as Sean chain-smoked and continued to 'unload'. I don't think we said more than a couple of dozen words over that period, but that was fine with us as we knew he just needed to get things off his chest. We had a special bonding time with Sean; gave him some titbits of advice; told him that God loved him right there in the middle of his mess. We wrapped our arms around this tough-looking, scary, young man and prayed with him while tears ran down his weathered cheeks. Man that was such an enriching experience. We have no idea of the outcome, just that we were grateful to have been 'planted' beside the river on that day so Sean could sort out some of his shit and ride away with renewed energy and determination to make some positive changes in his life.

* * *

Speaking of Victorian adventures, we got a real treat from a random stranger called Kettle whilst camping along the river, east of Orbost. Kettle lived on a property further down the road from where we had stopped to spend a couple of nights. We'd found a spot with a good feel about it and were scavenging around the nearby bush for some wood to light a fire and cook our dinner on, when Kettle and a friend drove past in her ute and honked her horn to say 'hello'. The next morning Kettle's ute appeared again, coming up the road in the other direction. She pulled in, jumped out of the cab and introduced herself. 'People round here call me Kettle', she said as she climbed up into the back of her ute and began to unload enough firewood to cook our dinners for a week and have a bonfire – BYO marshmallows! She had seen us - two perfect strangers - foraging for wood and had gone home, filled her ute and brought it back for us. What a blessing! With all that wood we were able to cook and stay warm and comfortable, but more than that, our hearts were warmed by Kettle's random generosity. You know that feeling when someone shows you unexpected kindness and you are just left feeling all warm and fuzzy inside?

It was so funny really, because the firewood scenario is an ongoing thing for us. One day, earlier on in our journey, we had arrived at a campsite just on dark – which we soon discovered was a really bad idea as it makes setting up camp and collecting wood a pain in the bum. To our surprise we found that someone had stacked wood beside a fireplace ready for the next weary traveller – hello, that would be us! We were so inspired by this simple and very practical act of kindness that we decided to do the same wherever we went. So now, before driving away from a campsite, we stack a small amount of wood beside the fireplace. It only takes us an extra ten minutes or so, but we know first-hand what a blessing it can be. We had been leaving these small piles of wood here and there, and then a week's worth of wood is dumped on us via a kind soul named Kettle. It may only be a simple thing but it just goes to prove that saying about 'sowing and reaping' is true. That particular saying comes from the bible in Galatians, where we are warned not to deceive or delude ourselves - a person will always reap what they sow.

If you would allow me the indulgence, I've got another wood story for you. Step loves to whittle away time on the road by whittling wood. He's always on the lookout for tree-branches that will make good walking-sticks, and when he finds one that he likes, he cuts it to the right size and sands it back until it is nice and smooth. Then he rubs it down with linseed oil or the like to bring out the individual features within the grain of the wood. He has made dozens of walking sticks this way and, being a perfectionist, they are real works of art. He loves to give them away to people we meet along our journey (some have gone to Indigenous elders and others to folk who aren't getting around as easily as they used to). Like leaving wood beside a fireplace, it is only a simple thing, but it blesses so many people. It thrills me to see the surprise and gratitude on people's faces when they receive an unexpected gift.

Twentieth Century Christian teacher, leader and author Watchman Nee said, 'I've never met a soul who set out to satisfy the Lord, who wasn't satisfied themself.' We get such a sense of purpose by thinking up creative ways to share what we have. Leaving wood at campsites ready for someone else's comfort or picking up rubbish in each town we visit comes from our philosophy to attempt to leave a place better than how we found it. It's often tiny things that many people might not even notice, but it leaves our hearts beating with the pulse of purpose. We know we are just a tiny piece in this crazy jigsaw we call life, but it all fits together to make an eternal difference.

We were served by a young girl in a pizza restaurant in Tumbarumba during our time on an orchard there. She was a dear young thing (doesn't that make me sound like an oldie) and as we got chatting she told us how she was working extra shifts to save enough money to go to India and volunteer in an orphanage for three months. Step and I both had the same inspiring thought at once... and, after a nod of approval to one another, we simply slipped her some money. Her eyes were as wide as the pizza trays on the wall behind her. It was so beautiful. She told us the amount of money we gave her would pay for her dinners every night of the three months of her stay. It was a simple gesture; and it just so happens someone from Wagga had blessed us with some money, so we were merely passing it on, or 'playing it forward' as my friend Elsie likes to say.

Recently we heard of a couple who own a motor-mechanics business in the Northern Beaches area of Sydney who do up second-hand cars and give them away to struggling, single-parents. Hooley-dooley, that's generous, and genius, don't you think? It doesn't have to be something as grand as giving away cars though. What have you got? We can all be generous in our own way – all we have to do is be willing to share our gifts, talents and resources with others. Remember, 'God loves a cheerful giver', and he's more than happy to put some SUPER into our NATURAL if we're prepared to step out in giving and serving.

* * *

For many years I used to wake up and wander aimlessly through the day. Now I try to wake up on purpose. You know what I mean? Don't just let your day happen to you; open your eyes and your heart and expect a day of meaning and purpose; look for the supernatural – it's happening all around us and we can tap into it. One thing I know for sure is that you won't be bored. You may even have all sorts of crazy experiences that really give you, and others, a new lease on life. You will be the giver and the receiver of some great stuff that can change the world - even if it is only one person at a time!

There's a story of a woman walking along a beach, and as she meanders along she notices that countless starfish have been washed up on the sand with the high tide, and are now in danger of dying. One at a time she begins to pick up the starfish and return them to the ocean. She repeats this over and over again, all the while being watched by a young fisherman. Finally the young man comes over and says, 'What difference is that going to make, there must be thousands of starfish washed up on this beach?' Without stopping to answer she picks up still another one and walks towards the water. As she tosses it into the ocean she turns to the man and replies, 'It certainly made a difference to that one.' Simple, random acts of kindness to one needy soul can change the world. As you go about life, I challenge you to look outside of yourself and to be conscious of your ability to help someone, anyone, even in a small way. Rather than always looking to be on the receiving end of things, why not become a giver.

I love to think bigger than just my circumstances (well, most of the time that is), and I wonder what it would look like if all of us reading this book reached out every day to one person; and that one person then joined us and began to reach out to one other person. With that sort of ripple-effect, as all of us are being blessed and being a blessing, it wouldn't be too long before the world was a different place, don't you think? Couldn't we change the world through kindness? If you break it down it's even more powerful to consider: If 50 people each did one hour of kindness during the week; that would amount to more than a full working-week's worth of kindness, with nobody doing more than one hour each. What if the 50 people that we bless decide to bless another 50 people? I need my number one son – he loves maths – he would be figuring out exactly what impact this would have over a month or a year. I reckon it would be tens of thousands, even millions of people impacted! The beauty is that nobody would have to bust their butt, just do their little bit to make it a reality. Kisses from heaven - it inspires me.

That reminds me of a cool t-shirt I spied a while back; on the front it said, 'Evil flourishes when good people do nothing'; and on the back it said, 'DO SOMETHING!!'

CHAPTER THREE
apples to pick

Inevitably, our financial situation fluctuates on our meandering journey around Oz, and things don't always work out as we think they should. Maybe it's because we 'camp out' until our money is all but gone before we get serious about boosting the bank balance. As our finances dwindle we're forced to look for work, ANY work. This one time we were told that we could easily get work picking apples at Batlow in NSW, so we made our way to Batlow, a town with a population of about 1,450. With high levels of faith and low levels of funds we arrived in town at 5.10 one afternoon and started thinking about somewhere to camp for the night. We found a 'rest area' beside the highway but it turned out to be a dud – nothing but an old picnic table without running water, let alone any essential bladder-releasing facilities, if you catch my drift.

We drove on, and seeing there were a number of orchards along the road, we stopped in to see whether they were looking for pickers. We explained that we were desperate for work, trying hard to side-step the fact that we had never picked an apple in our lives, except in the fruit and veg section of 'Woolies'. 'Sorry guys we have all the pickers we need at the moment; why don't you try so and so down the road?' wasn't what we wanted to hear. So away we went again, hopeful that the next place would be different. 'We've just finished the 'red dels' and it's going to be another week before the 'grannies' are ready for picking' was the disappointing reply. We hadn't anticipated that it would be quite so hard to get work when the pamphlets said it was smack in the middle of picking season. We were learning fast that things don't always work out the way you think they ought to. These orchard owners explained they had pickers lined up for when the apples were ready, but we could give them a call if nothing else came up for us. We found a roadside fruit stall, and a kind lady named Anne gave us a few inside tips.

We were just about out of food so we shopped as sensibly as we could at the local IGA store, spending $16.70 on supplies we hoped would feed us for a few days. We met Angelique, a backpacking French lady who was travelling Oz on the 'harvest trail' – picking fruit wherever and whenever it was seasonal. She introduced us to a local named Jenna, who phoned a friend, Lauren, who worked at the co-op. We had a little party together, celebrating our upcoming breakthrough. Hubby and I then found a spot to camp with a great view overlooking Batlow. Feeling elated at the many 'chance' meetings along the way, we made a fire, cooked dinner and settled in for the night. Batlow was proving a very friendly town.

By 8.15 the following morning we were out and about searching for more leads and following up on those we already had. We filled in forms for work at the co-op and talked to people in the hardware store, library and caravan parks. By ten o'clock we had a list of names and phone numbers.

Step poached some eggs and cooked toast on our gas burner in Reedy Creek Park while I phoned some work contacts. The park proved an interesting stop, as it was the sight of the first Olympic swimming pool, built in 1934. There were photos of swimming carnivals that were held back then with schools coming from all over the area – from Tumut, Cootamundra, Gundagai, Junee and Wagga. By the time brunch had been packed away we had received six negatives on the work front.

By 1.30pm it had begun to pour so we tucked ourselves up in bed in Buzz, parked in a cul-de-sac beside a sports ground where a holly tree was growing healthily. This is the only holly tree I have seen in the wild so I had to mention it. I don't recall seeing a holly tree before so I was taken aback. I have drawn and painted them for Christmas gifts, but don't recall actually seeing a real-life tree with those distinctive sharp leaves and bunches of red berries. Batlow may not have produced work for us thus far, but it had provided a beautiful holly tree for me to marvel over... and it wasn't even Christmas. It was probably closer to Easter than Christmas.

We'd been told the apple orchid owners were waiting on the heat to break and a cold spell to arrive so their apples could be picked in perfect conditions, so the deafening thunder of rain on our van's roof brought us hope that it could be the beginning of an opportunity to work. The temperature had dropped markedly since the morning's glorious sunshine.

The librarian we visited the next day was definitely not your typical librarian. She wasn't old, wrinkled or sporting horn-rimmed glasses and a tight grey bun. She kindly gave us a list of another 20 orchards to contact. It was Step's turn to make some calls - leaving messages on answering machines or thanking the owners for considering us. None of the calls proved to be fruitful (sic). All we needed was one opportunity to start work and we'd be springing into action with bells on.

It was cold and raining again so we were confined to Buzz, tucked warmly under the bedcovers for the remainder of that day. Since being on the road, hubby manages to fall asleep wherever we are, so he was stacking zeds beside me while I was scanning through our lists. It was a far-cry from our dream of a carefree life of luxury on the road.

I thought we'd arrive in Batlow to the same greeting we had received in Healesville Victoria, where we had volunteered in the wake of the tragic Black Saturday fires of February 2009. We zoomed into that smoke-filled town in Buzz and offered our services to a chorus of 'thank God you're here' just like the comedy series of the same name. There were cheers all round. Though, unlike the television show, it wasn't at all funny. The time we spent there was a humbling experience as we served families who had lost loved ones, homes, livelihoods, pets, livestock, and everything but the clothes on their backs. Most days were stinking hot with an eerie, smoky heat-haze hovering over the town. Almost every day there was talk of the possibility of evacuating the entire town, and every second day there was a meeting held at the local park, where the chief of the CFA (country fire authority) would bring the latest updates and predictions. At the peak of the fires there were literally hundreds and hundreds of volunteer fire fighters from all over the country assembled in one of the local sporting areas, with some coming from New Zealand and the United States as well. We were in awe of these brave men and women. I'll never forget the sight of them heading out just after dawn, and again at sunset. They formed a massive convoy of trucks and tankers that were too many to count, heading out into the most treacherous conditions, barely able to see or breathe as the dense smoke hung forebodingly over everything, everywhere. Sometimes we saluted them, and other times we were brought to tears at the sight.

We didn't have much to offer, but we were able to help at one of the many Relief Centres that had been set up to support those who had lost so much. We spent months in one of the centres distributing the bare essentials like food, clothes, personal-hygiene products, tools, etc. We heard many heartbreaking stories, and hugged lots of broken people who were overwhelmed by the daunting prospect of rebuilding their lives. Some people had literally escaped with what they were wearing and nothing else.

Church services were held regularly to encourage the survivors, and to help people deal with what they had lost. We made many friends – fellow volunteers and some victims of the devastation the fires brought through those once sleepy, pretty towns. The people were in desperate need and we were without commitments or time limits, we had nowhere else we needed to be, and we had nothing to drag us away. It was one of those times when being on the road really felt like it was exactly what we were meant to be doing. We could not have stayed there helping in Healesville for so long if it hadn't been for our friends and family back home who were supporting us by randomly depositing funds into our bank account to meet our needs. It was a team effort. Most great successes in life are like that. There isn't a soul on earth who doesn't need a helping hand at times.

* * *

The Batlow picture looked nothing like we predicted – we were holed-up in our van in the cold and rain with no money and zero work. Time passes very slowly under such circumstances. There are only so many books you can read and so much love-making you can do. We hadn't had a hot shower in over a month. We probably stank to high heaven to outsiders, but we usually managed to set up a bush-shower or find a stream to 'bathe' in most days. Tepid water in a plastic washing-up tub was what we resorted to on more than one occasion.

Leann, one of my friends featuring throughout this book, had phoned me asking how things were going, and I answered whilst shaving my legs squatted over said plastic washing-up tub. She asked whether our dishes were washed *after* my shave or before. She had a scary vision of everything coming out all furry, just like your lap after a good cat-patting session (No, my sweater is not cashmere, it is *catmere*). Some people might think that's gross but that's just reality on the road. To be honest though, the answer to Leann's question is somewhere in-between. We fill the tub with water, we clean the dishes, we change the water, we bathe, we change the water, we wash the dishes again – and so the pattern is repeated, over and over - unless there is a river or ocean available of course – and then the tub is exclusively for dishes. Phew, nice to clarify that one; though I know you are still screwing up your nose in disapproval. I can hear you thinking, 'no matter how much rinsing you do, that system is just wrong; it would be like peeing in the same hand basin that you wash your face in.'

Confession time: I had to do that once. I was staying in a cheap hotel in one of Australia's better known cities, and I had a tiny room filled with nothing more than a single bed and a basin. Communal bathroom facilities were down the hallway, a turn to the left and then a sharp turn to the right. About 3am I was laying wide-awake, which is pretty standard for me, and there was a hell of a commotion outside in the hallway. I had to pee real bad but the thought of venturing down the hallway past whoever was making all that racket, made me feel a tad vulnerable. I was thinking, 'What red-blooded Aussie male wouldn't want to ravish me, what with my sexy flannelette nightie, fluffy slippers, and serious bed-hair sticking out at all angles.' In the end it was my bladder that forced the issue. It began to warn me that it was time for release... 'if you can't tackle those men outside, it's either the bed or the basin.' You know the rest. I felt totally justified.

* * *

Meanwhile, back in Buzz in Batlow... the prospect of finding not only work, but somewhere comfortable to stay, somewhere with hot running water and toilets, wasn't looking good. Despite feeling a little down, we talked our faith up by remembering moments of miraculous provision in the past.

We spent the next three days without word from anyone. Do you know how long three days can be? The rain continued to fall and our mood could have matched the weather had we not upheld each other with words of affirmation and confirmation of God's goodness and provision, or was it that we were just not speaking to one another? A door would be opened for us somewhere, hopefully real soon. I recall our jubilation when we were out on a walk one day and happened to find some wild apple trees growing along the old railway line. We ate so many apples that day we thought all our Christmases had come at once. We agreed that even if work never came we could always say we had picked apples in Batlow ha-ha. We journeyed up to the Look Out, a popular spot to enjoy dinner, but the rain was relentless. We met a couple of backpackers, again from France, Emanuel and Francis, and together we shared tinned-soup with added bacon pieces (from us), and couscous with peanuts and dates (from them). We talked and laughed as we huddled tightly together under the tiny awning of Buzz, pretending we weren't getting wet.

The following morning's sunshine allowed us to dry some of the gear that had been drenched the previous night, and as we looked down on the town below there was a tangible air of celebration as the annual show was getting underway, complete with carnival-rides and side-shows. We would have joined in the fun, but as we had run out of money, the five dollar entry fee was a bit rich for us. Every now and again we could hear the ringmaster's voice booming out and floating up from his loudspeaker on the wind, luring us down to view what we could around the showground complex. We loved the sense of community, of coming together, that the annual show provoked.

The sun brought little warmth to the chilly autumn day, and although we were without fuel or money, the French guys from the night before had left us a heart-warming gift of chestnuts and walnuts, gathered from the orchard where they had been working. We were always grateful for small blessings, but our situation was becoming desperate. We needed a miracle.

Dennis became our miracle. He phoned us out of the blue and asked us to begin picking that afternoon. It was finally happening. He explained how we could get to his orchard in Tumbarumba, and a whole new journey began.

Upon arrival, Dennis introduced us to his son Warren, and we were given a quick instruction session on picking techniques; what to do, and what not to do. After being handed a 'joey-pouch' each (our picking bags), we were led to the unending rows of apple trees. Before we knew it, we were picking apples - for real this time. We set ourselves a goal to fill four bins of apples throughout the afternoon, and had achieved our goal by around 5.30 – a great effort for our first half day. In typical Step fashion, when I quit after four bins, he began a fifth. 'We've still got another hour of daylight,' he protested. The joey pouch had made me a bit sore and I could feel my back muscles protesting. My writing fingers (I had to write by hand in journals throughout this time as we had no electricity for our laptops) were more than a little worse for wear. Bandaids-on-every-finger-for-the-first-two-weeks kind of 'worse for wear', but otherwise all was good. It didn't take us long to catch on to picking and binning the apples without bruising them, and it felt great to be part of such a big production. The father and son were very friendly and encouraging, and we instantly clicked with them.

That first day, when our bins were collected by Warren as he did the rounds in his tractor, he informed us that he had checked our apples and they were all OK (phew, not bruised and battered like some other gung-ho pickers), so we had work with him for the season if we wanted it. IF we wanted it; we were over the moon; we were desperadoes. Dennis kindly directed us to his farmhouse and paid us straight up for our four bins, which enabled us to duck into town to make some purchases to keep us going until payday. Before we showered or had a chance to massage our aching backs, we were speeding into town to make sure we caught the shops before they closed. Oh, it felt sooooo good. That small amount of money felt like all the riches of the world in our hands. We were King and Queen again. We were world conquerors and the road ahead of us was paved with gold. We purchased the essentials, AND a sizzling prawn and garlic pizza. We were back in the land of the living.

Upon returning later that night we were assigned our little camp spot at the orchard. There was a communal shower and toilet block, with hot running water. It felt like heaven to us. Now, when I say 'heaven', I use the term very loosely. The communal block with its concrete floor that flooded with every shower, was shared by men and women alike. It also housed the one shared fridge, the one sink for washing dishes or faces (not peeing); and the dunny doors were so small they exposed all but the barest essentials to anyone who walked into the room. But we managed to overlook those minor (if not revealing) details, as we had money, food, hot water and work. Yeah, we were in heaven.

The very next day we were up early and proudly picked eight bins between us. Over the next few months we picked many different varieties of apples, pacing ourselves, finding our groove. Wait, best I am completely honest with you here, I paced myself, but hubby, like most men, couldn't be outdone by the other super-pickers, so he would continue to pick for another hour or two after I'd knocked off for the day. I would lie back in my camp chair, enthroned like a princess upon my purple cushions, and write, occasionally looking up to watch him while he sweated away in the heat to pick an extra couple of bins.

During our work-breaks throughout the day we would share salami sandwiches, a laugh, and a carry-on with the other pickers, crazy, cheeky Warren, and the tractor drivers. We particularly loved the evenings where many of the pickers would sit around our fire and chat and joke and relax together. We got to share life with these people, and we were focused on trying to encourage and help anyone who needed it. We had many a laugh as we educated some of the 'Frenchies' in Aussie language and culture; 'No, Australian is nothing like proper English!' A month in and we were becoming rather feral with Step's curls morphing into dreadlocks, and our bodies darkening in the sun and becoming more sinewy and toned through the constant hard work. After getting down to our last dollars, we were very appreciative of the money we were earning. We did our best to make hay while the sun was still shining; and we continued to look for ways to live out our purpose and share the 'loving vibes' with people.

We made some good friends during our time on the orchard, some of whom we are still in contact. We returned to the same orchard the following year to do it all over again. Back we went, to pick apples by day - red and green, large and small, climbing into thick, triffid-like trees and trellised vine-like trees. We climbed, laboured over and under, and picked every last apple. We shared around the camp fires of an evening; and showered behind nothing but a torn, billowing nylon curtain, while the French apple-pickers washed their dishes in the communal sink and another strained to release his bowels behind one of the tiny lavatory doors.

CHAPTER FOUR
short skirt

An essential element to being the best you possibly can be is to actually *like* yourself. Man, this was a tough lesson for me. I used to mope around like my life was an apology – like a quivering dog walking in fear of rejection. My life was meant to be a statement, not an apology. I am a hand-crafted masterpiece. Yet that kind of self-talk doesn't always come naturally. I used to loathe myself... enough to want to harm myself and attempt to take my life. Now, I like being me. I really enjoy being a woman. I am thrilled to be a participating member of the female race and the human race. I enjoy the many roles I have - mum, wife, friend, sister, daughter, motivator, work-colleague, writer, etc.

I have a past. A past filled with all sorts of yucky stuff that I'd prefer to forget. I had serious dramas at home, at school and at the boarding school I was later sent to. I had addictions, suicidal thoughts and attempted suicide. I was sexually assaulted as an early teen, had an unwanted pregnancy before I was married, and have experienced both homelessness and rejection. I have been jobless and money-less, and have had a marriage break down, and thankfully, a restoration. I know what it is to feel helpless and hopeless. You think I want to sit around all day dwelling or 'brooding' on those things? Heck no!

I've been pulled up out of the mud. My feet have been set upon solid rock. I know who I am, and I dare to dream. It has been a process - sometimes a painful process - but the rewards have outweighed the pain, and the journey has made me a better person (I hope). Forgiveness, of myself and others, and love are very powerful tools. Not many things in life feel quite as good, and fill a heart with hope, like having the chance to start again with a CLEAN SLATE. I don't know what you have been through. But God does! And he says, if you allow him to, he will 'keep you so busy enjoying life that you'll take no time to brood over the past' (that's a quote from Ecclesiastes).

I remember watching Australian Idol on television during the 2009 season at my youngest daughter's home one night (we don't own a television; it's not one of the essentials when you live in a bed-on-wheels, so occasionally we gatecrash other peoples' lounge rooms to get our TV fix). If you missed the series, here's my angle on it - Australian Idol was basically a glorified talent quest where young people-come-entertainers would subject themselves to all manner of criticism and ridicule, in the hope of winning the competition, gaining idol status and a big fat recording deal. They performed in front of a panel of judges and a live studio audience, and would often come into the competition quite raw, with plenty of rough edges needing to be knocked off. Over the duration of the show, which was a few months, each contestant was groomed by professional coaches, until one by one they were voted-off or eliminated. The last one standing, so to speak, became Australia's Idol and supposedly then went on to fame and fortune and a glorious future in the entertainment industry.

Anyway, I was watching the show one September evening and a little European girl, who was obviously no stranger to stage performance - you know the type - all big, spoofy black hair with huge eyes and pouty lips – came on. Speaking of pouty lips, how cool are Mick Jaggers' lips! I reckon if Mick Jagger wanted to kiss me in public I'd just have to let him, and then of course, turn the other cheek, as any good Christian girl should.

Where was I? Oh, the young European girl. She was moving and grooving and shaking and filling the stage with her dynamic presence. I can't remember too many details, but she did have a short skirt and great legs.

So, when this little European girl from Australian Idol had finished her performance, one of the judges commented, 'it is difficult to judge you because I can't tell who you are; you seem all about the 'show". I just loved her reply – and because it was years ago, I am paraphrasing, 'I perform with enthusiasm because I'm an enthusiastic person. I perform with energy because I'm energetic. I perform with excitement because I'm a naturally excitable person. What you see IS who I am.' Woohoo! Bam! Go girl! Someone who knows who she is, and makes no apologies for it. The studio audience cheered in admiration, and those sitting around the television in my daughter's lounge room joined in.

Hey, speaking of a short skirt and great legs... this one time when I was out with my three daughters, about eight years back or more, I was wearing one of my infamous short skirts, (a Chrissy trademark), and I said to my girls, 'What am I going to do when I'm an old lady still wearing mini-skirts?' And I couldn't believe what they said... IN UNISON. 'Mum! You are an old lady wearing mini-skirts!' So damn rude (and honest) I could've slapped them. But I guess, looking on the bright side, the pressure is off me now. I have already crossed the line; I AM mutton dressed as lamb! It looks like I have taken care of that bridge – and burnt it – leaving me free to just go with it. And, really, if you saw my legs, you would understand why I just have to show them off.

I was speaking at a Women's Breakfast about two years ago and I had brought along a beautiful pink and black skirt to give away. It was a small size, a tiny item of clothing that didn't involve much material. I began by holding it up for the women to see how pretty it was. It really was cute and I had bought it on a whim. You see, after taking it home I had discovered that I had been dreaming - as I couldn't do up the zip at the back. Since when was I a size 'small'? (Well, since you asked, truth be told, it was many years ago ... coming to grips with my broadening middle is just part of the aforementioned struggle I have living in my own time warp.) My mummy-tummy (always blame it on the children) was a tad rounder than I liked to admit. But I had figured that it was a pretty skirt, and I had paid a decent price for it as far as op-shop bargains go, surely it wouldn't matter if it didn't exactly fit me?

Being the clever fashion guru that I am, I had simply left the zip undone, folded the top of the skirt over, and popped on a long free-flowing shirt over the top – surely no one would notice. There are all sorts of wardrobe tricks available to the desperate, but during the one and only brief time I had worn it the week before, my eldest daughter's eldest daughter had looked at me with her nose all scrunched up and her head cocked to one side, and told me my petticoat was hanging out. I informed her that Granny's skirt had been designed to look like that. When I walked into my daughter's kitchen where my hubby was preparing me a meal (fortunately his love language is service so he cooks most of our meals – and even more fortunately my love expression is to allow him to serve me, ha-ha), he looked at me with a strange look on his face. Cocking his head sideways he sized up my rear end, and told me that my petticoat was hanging out. I raised my eyebrows as though addressing an imbecile, informing him that the two-tiered skirt was all the fashion.

Let me tell you now, that it is good to check yourself out after two people have observed a wardrobe malfunction. I was at a party that fateful evening, when I caught my reflection in a mirror HALF WAY THROUGH THE NIGHT, and too late, realised the outer black cotton of the dress was all scrunched up from my butt being too large for it, and the pink nylon material was hanging limply well below the outer material. It was an atrocious sight. I am not sure how my hubby had allowed me out of the house looking that way. What WAS he thinking! So I had taken the skirt with me, held it up at this Women's Breakfast and asked a young, (scrawny), princess to come and collect it, it was hers now, I was blessing her with it. The women laughed and applauded my generosity, but under my breath I told this gorgeous waif that if she ever wore it while I was around, I would scratch her eyes out.

* * *

'To enjoy your work and accept your lot in life, this is indeed a gift from God. God keeps such people so busy enjoying life that they take no time to brood over the past' - that's Ecclesiastes 5:20 I mentioned earlier. It says accepting who you are is a gift from God. That young girl on Idol knew her gift was to enjoy life and to do her best to share her gift with others. The verse concludes with 'God keeps such people so busy enjoying life that they take no time to brood over the past.' Who keeps us busy enjoying life? God does. I reckon the bible, which is certainly NOT that boring out-dated book I used to think it was, continuously reminds us to forget the crap and the dirt that may have been piled upon us in the past. 'Don't brood over it,' but keep pushing through it, and rise above it. That's maturity and contentment.

A couple of months ago on Facebook I noticed, Leann, (one of my inner-circle girlfriends I mentioned earlier) issued an 'encouragement challenge', to see if her friends could out-encourage one another. What a competition, eh? It had us all going. We rose to the challenge and filled page after page with words of encouragement, all striving to outdo one another. You know that when you encourage someone you are actually helping them grow in confidence, hope and courage to do what they were created for – it literally means 'imparting courage into'. I think everyone ended up winners through that little exercise.

If you feel that you have been held back or kept down by discouragement, begin to appreciate who you are and where you are planted. Focus on the positives in your life – you can work on goals to improve your situation much easier from a positive position. You know, I reckon it even goes further than that, maybe, just maybe, we can't work on goals from any position other than a positive one. I'll leave that thought with you.

I got an email last month from a woman I used to work with many moons ago. It read, 'Chrissy, you would be so proud of me. I have quit smoking and I've lost weight, and it's all because I realised the gorgeous woman I am.' Is that the best email to receive ever? What a great revelation. I loved the way she began, 'Chrissy, you would be so proud of me'. In all the years we had worked together, I had constantly tried to encourage her. Yet, no matter what I said, she always had a negative comeback. 'But I'm overweight.' 'My hair needs re-doing.' You know the drill. Sometimes, when we are in a low place or negative space, we simply cannot receive compliments. We simply WON'T believe there is anything good about ourselves. So when she began her email in that way I knew instantly that she had finally got it. She had 'accepted her place in life', and she began to get busy enjoying it, and through that, was empowered to take responsibility for her own happiness instead of making excuses or 'brooding over the past'.

And she is right – I AM proud of her!

Though my knowledge of the Hebrew language is extremely limited, I have learned that the Hebrew word for enjoy contains the suggestion of dancing, leaping, spinning around with intense emotion, to rejoice, to be glad and bring joy to yourself and others. And in Zephaniah the bible says that God sings a love song over us, with exuberance. He rejoices over you with gladness. How does that make you feel? Are you getting excited and enthusiastic yet? Are you enjoying feeling exuberant - electrified? Has your world been enhanced? Enjoying the 'E' words? (My vocabulary in my early days was filled with the 'F' word, and I am certainly glad I have stepped up from there. 'E' is much more entertaining!)

One day, when our kids were really little, our middle daughter came running in to tattle-tale on her four-year-old brother, who was trailing forlornly behind her. 'Mum, mum,' she was yelling in horror, 'He said the 'F' word!' Our faces and hearts sank. By now our other children had gathered around to see what sort of punishment would be dealt to match such a heinous crime. To clarify the situation, so we could make a fair assessment, we asked what had happened. You should have seen our faces when it turned out he had said FART. Fart was the 'F' word. We had a good chuckle over that one.

We had a bit of a laugh over an 'E' word once, too. Again, back when the kids were little and everything in their world was filled with wonder and fascination and dobbing one another in, one of them was indignant over being called the 'E' word by their sister. We couldn't for the life of us figure out what the 'E' word was, until one of the kids enlightened us, 'She called me an idiot.' I guess it does sound like an 'E' word. Do you remember The Ren and Stimpy Show, that off-colour, slapstick cartoon show that ran after school hours during the 1990s? Ren, the emotionally unstable Chihuahua became well-known for his line to the dim-witted cat, 'you eediot Stimpy.' 'Idiot' was definitely an 'E' word on that program.

Yeah, real 'E' words are better! I reckon we should be getting excited too. If it's good enough for God, it's good enough for me, right? And I don't think it should stop there – how about dancing, jumping, twirling, twisting, boogying and raising our hands and wiggling our bums (even if our bums are hanging out of a black and pink mini-skirt). But some people just won't allow themselves to get stirred up. When hubby and I were out western NSW, many of the young Indigenous girls were embarrassed about getting excited or even seen to be getting excited. One of the most common words on their lips was 'shame'. They said it about everything, from their hair and clothes, to a guy driving down the street looking their way. They were trapped in a paralysing belief that left them daring to do nothing. These girls were beautiful, yet they lived in shame. They were so held back by it that they wouldn't try anything, or allow themselves to get excited at all. The bondage these girls were in, broke my heart. It certainly wasn't what they had been designed for.

CHAPTER FIVE
chooks

Something we have to realise before we go any further is that any time we genuinely choose to move forward we will face opposition. Sooner or later, regardless of how prepared we are, obstacles ARE going to get in the way. That's just life.

Life should be viewed as a long-distance race, not a sprint. Some people are always in a mad rush, aren't they? They run up your heels with their shopping trolley if you get in their way; they tap their feet and roll their eyes when the person in front of them at the checkout asks for a price check (admittedly, that can really bug you). They are the same ones who overtake you in their car on unbroken lines with no regard for anyone's safety. They are on a mission, in a big hurry, and the rest of the world can just move out of their damn way!

I have told you that I learn things the hard way, and one thing I know for sure is that life isn't a sprint race. We need to learn to pace ourselves. It's about enjoying the journey, not just focusing on our grand arrival to utopia. It isn't helpful to drive ourselves to the point of exhaustion and collapse. Before I learnt my tough lesson on living a balanced life, I was so busy doing stuff, everything became one big nightmarish blur – and I have a feeling, a bit of an inkling, that someone reading this has just gone 'ouch'!

So, back to this long-distance race – our own private ultra-marathon, if you like. We are runners, we are athletes, and therefore we need to train. Training needs to be balanced. We need to run, work, rest, eat and play in a BALANCED way so we can achieve our goals while living out our amazing lives and being the best us we can be. Here's another saying that comes to mind, compliments of my dad who heard it from his dad, who probably heard it from his, 'All work and no play makes Jack a dull boy'. I have to agree. And if you've ever heard stories about Jesus, you will know that he taught us through example that he agrees too... he went off to quiet places to rest, pray and recharge. He spent time with his mates, always had time and energy for others, and he enjoyed the odd party. He knew his purpose in life and he knew what he needed to do to fulfil it without losing his joy. Another saying from my repertoire goes like this, 'if you don't chill out, you'll burn out!' I'm unsure where that saying came from, but it sounds like something my eldest daughter says, 'Chillax mum!'

As I was about to tell you before I rudely interrupted myself, prolific English writer HG Wells poses an interesting question, 'What on earth would people do with themselves if something didn't stand in their way?' Call it what you want - poo, dirt or adversity - but it CAN be our friend, if we allow it to. We can use each obstacle to teach us more about our strengths and weaknesses, to make us wiser and to build endurance. Be warned though, people will be jealous and threatened by a person on the move; a person living with conviction and purpose. Don't let others' negativity swamp you in a sea of doubt. Our courage and conviction will inspire some and offend others. That's just human nature. We can't control other people's reactions, but we can keep a tight rein on our own thinking and actions. We need to carry our dreams close to our hearts, and be careful who we share them with. We need to seek out 'safe' people to share our treasures.

I was sitting with our eldest son and my hubby one day (safe people in my life) in our son's unit in Newcastle NSW. We were talking about our goals and dreams. I asked my hubby and son, 'What do you think some of my weaknesses and strengths are?' Now, that's a dangerous question, and you have to be in a pretty good space to cope with an honest answer – fortunately I was at the time. We listed some of my strengths as *writing, motivational speaking* and *encouragement*. I am a real *people-person*. I love being surrounded by people - building them up and seeing them laugh. Laughter is great for the soul and brings such freedom. As author Mary Pettibone Poole says, 'She who laughs, lasts.'

Now, these were my strengths we were noting. My *obvious* strengths that came to our minds quickly. I am pretty confident that my hubby and son had some of my obvious weaknesses in mind, but went about them a bit more diplomatically... best to ease into that stuff. My son said something profound. He said, 'Mum, sometimes a strength can be a weakness.' I nodded politely, but awaited clarification. He went on to explain while socialising is a good thing, spending too much time with others when I should be working on my latest book or preparing for a speaking engagement, could distract me from pursuing my goals.

Hang on; allow me to digress for a moment. I was not always an other-centred kind of gal with a desire to help people. Far from it. That's why I am writing this book. For the first 20 years of my life I was not a nice person. I was an awful, spiteful and angry person actually, and, because I was hurting within myself, I would hurt others around me. 'Hurt people hurt people', as the saying goes.

Anyway, my hubby and son kindly had some other things to add about my weaknesses, but I had tuned out by then, ha-ha. They helped me face some home-truths that I'd probably been side-stepping for years. They said that I could be undisciplined with time management; had a tendency to put difficult things in the 'too hard' basket; and could be haphazard with organising certain areas of my life. An example would be my broken mobile phone, the one with the shattered screen, that I want magically fixed. But the thought of contending with the young people who work at my local phone network office who speak in a totally different language, straight from some cyberspace, data dictionary that nobody has bothered to introduce me to, freaks the life out of me. Another example is my lack of follow-through with my writing. Two of my novels, that spanned a period of five years of spasmodic writing, one of 60,000 words and one of 90,000 words, were never edited or published. (I must admit the novels were pretty crap anyway, so not so great a loss as one might think.)

I am in the process of learning that *discipline* and *organisation* are essentials for achieving goals. *Denial* and *wishing* don't really cut it in the real world... not if you want to live a life of purpose. Without discipline and organisation we can sometimes feel like we are chooks running around with our heads cut off. Have you ever actually seen that happen? To a chook, I mean?

We used to have a farm when our children were young, and on that farm we had some chooks (almost like a song, isn't it? E-i-e-i-o). These chooks had a couple of purposes - to provide us with eggs, and, if they weren't able to do that, to provide us with roast chicken dinners. Every now and again, when the number of chooks got too great for our yard, or we had too many roosters strutting and pushing their weight around and fighting one another, we would have a killing day. Gosh, that sounds terrible, doesn't it! We would gather the 'chosen ones' from the coop, and as my hubby would sharpen the axe, we would all stand around in anticipation. Then we would watch as he swung the axe down on the chicken's neck, severing the head from the body. It was a very sharp axe, and it would only involve one swift, strong, downward swing. He would let the chicken go and the body would then run around like crazy, staggering and running in circles, getting nowhere, until its lifeblood was drained and it would just flop to the ground, spent. I know people who live their lives like that! They are always running here and there and getting nowhere in a hurry, using all their energy on things of little consequence. Without a goal or destination in mind, they eventually end up just exhausted and worn out, and never really achieve anything.

I reckon we can learn a lot from our fine feathered friends. Over the years we've had lots of chooks, from fluffy little Silky-Bantams (that make great pets for the kids), to Rhode Island Reds, Barnevelders, Australorps, Light Sussex and White Leghorns. When I was growing up, it used to be common for families to have a chicken coop in their backyards. Of my five children, only one, my eldest daughter, keeps chooks – and they are purely egg-layers (maybe the group chook-killing sessions of their childhood put them off – possibly something for future counsellors to work through). This same daughter is the one, when about nine years old, informed her brothers and sisters that 'a doctor who cares for animals is called a vegetarian.' This daughter's three prolific layers of today are real family pets with names; Jack, Rosie and Lily. Yes, Jack is a hen, but who could tell when she was just a fluffy little ball of yellow and my six-year-old granddaughter declared 'him' Jack?!

One of my early experiences with chooks was when my mum took me to a distant uncle's property, which had rows and rows of iron sheds. Inside were **battery chooks**. This was a mass-production set-up, designed to gather the most eggs in the shortest time-frame despite the atrociously unhealthy conditions the hens were kept under. There were no roosters allowed, just rows and rows of tired, bedraggled hens. Pecking at layer-pellets and producing eggs was the lot of these bored hens, until they died. I think these battery chook sheds are illegal these days, or soon to be at least, thanks to the work of animal activists. These long, hot sheds had no natural lighting, just fluorescent lights to trick the hens into laying twice a day instead of once. It was all about maximum production. Their whole lives were spent in undersized cages and they were fed nothing but manufactured pellets. The pellets were placed in a tray at the front of the cage and their eggs dropped down into a tray at the back. These poor chooks' lives involved three things, and three things only - to eat, poo and lay eggs. They never saw the outside world; they were all work and no play; and had no opportunity to breed, or to meet their 'Mr Right' Rooster. Without fresh air, clean water and natural light their feathers would fall out and they would look sick and miserable. It was a shocking sight that I've never forgotten, the kind of stuff that gives you nightmares. I later learned that even as times changed and the cruelty of this type of 'farming' was questioned, those hens that were 'rescued' could not stand up, scratch or peck around like healthy chooks. Most had to be put down.

Another type of chook is the **caged chook**. These were the more familiar ones around the neighbourhood of my childhood. These had shelter and natural light, but remained inside the confines of their cages. They quickly devoured any worms or grass in the coop within the first week, and from then on spent most of their lives scratching in dirt and their own poo. They did have clean water and a varied diet, because they got to have the family's food scraps as well as mixed grains. They would squabble over the crumbs in the cage while all the time they could see green pastures of backyards that they could never get to enjoy. As a matter of fact, they became so accustomed to being locked in the cage that if you opened the door, they usually ran to the shelter of their enclosure and huddled together, afraid. Apart from the occasional rendezvous with the rooster, there was no interaction with other animals.

The third kind is the **free-range chooks**. Ah, an uncle of mine, dad's brother-in-law, had these. These were my favourites. My uncle was a friendly farmer who talked to his chooks and allowed them to roam freely on his property. The hens could partner with Mr Rooster any time they liked (or rather, any time the rooster liked); they could have chickens of their own and bring them up freely. The eggs these chooks produced were the healthiest and tastiest I have ever known. These chooks ate green grass, fresh worms and tasty, crunchy bugs; they had a deliciously diverse and healthy diet. They had a coop they could wander in-and-out of freely, enjoying shelter from the sun and protection from predators. They had it all, including warmth, natural light, fresh water, tall trees to roost in and a varied social life. They knew the other animals - the horse and the cow, the pigs and the geese, the dog and the cat, the ferret and the guinea pigs.

You might be feeling like one of the types of chooks mentioned here, and you might have just realised you are in the wrong cage! I reckon today might be a day to change cages or to set yourself free like the free-range chook. Unlike the chooks, we get to choose our cage. Do you want to be a battery hen that is all work and no play until you die? Are you content to be a caged chook where you can see life going on outside your cage, but you would rather run to the back of your shelter where you know it is safe, than get involved. You aren't meeting anyone or doing anything, but you feel 'safe'. You might be bored of your surroundings, your food and your limited company, but no way will you open the door and march into that lush, grassy backyard. Or do you want to be the farm free-range chook who proudly and happily produces eggs for the farmer and lives a balanced, interesting, exciting, expanding life? You really do have the choice. Come on, my free-range friend - I want to encourage you to come out and fly! Come out and LIVE!

I love this simple saying, 'Before you die, live'. Some people are so busy worrying, scurrying, planning and stressing, they forget they're actually living RIGHT NOW – not some time in the future, but right now.

* * *

Hubby and I have never been city-dwellers. We've always lived in the suburbs of larger towns or in small country towns, but never in the city. Once we had said goodbye to 'normal' life and hit the road in Buzz to travel this wonder-filled country, we continued to avoid cities. So, after we'd been on the road for six months or so, most of our time had been spent in even smaller towns or in the bush. Cities aren't really our scene, especially in Buzz, as there is nowhere to park and live comfortably in a bed-on-wheels. I recall heading into Melbourne after months of quietness and peace away from the hustle-bustle, and the contrast from life in the bush was mind-blowing.

We were staying in the unit our youngest daughter had been renting at the time. Though we had purchased a council permit to park our technicoloured Buzz on the busy street outside, we certainly couldn't live in it. We had grown so used to living outdoors that the walls of the unit were closing in on me and I was developing cabin fever. The weather had gone from cold to colder and the drizzling rain and bleakly, grey day outside did nothing to encourage me to leave the warmth and comforts of the unit.

Braving the elements, we jumped in Buzz, taking our notepads and pens with us (hubby is a writer too), and drove to where we could sit and spend some time watching and getting a feel for the city. We stopped in a one-hour parking zone that was soon to turn into a clearway. Everyone and everything seemed to be in a rush. The city seemed to have huge strong arms pushing and shoving people along at a hectic pace, propelling them ever onward and forward, faster and faster. Nothing was exempt; cars, trams, buses, pedestrians, joggers, shoppers, business-people - everything was under the city's powerful spell.

We began to feel that our contentment with the simple things of life was fading fast. Up until now we had been content with very little, but we suddenly wanted – needed – more. More clothes and accessories, new shoes, fancier foods, the latest CDs and computer software, and a host of other 'essentials'. The insatiable hunger of consumerism was devouring people's souls without them knowing it, and it was trying to get its claws into us. On the end of the city's huge arms were its large hands, hands that clutched at people's insides, dragging contentment out and forcing in desires for more. 'Take me, eat me, buy me, you need me, you're nothing without me,' the city teased. It was exhausting. The battle was intense. Even as I reassured myself of the delights of my simplistic lifestyle, conflict raged inside me. I was supposed to be an observer, not a participant.

Our quiet lifestyle in national parks - beside rivers, on beaches and within rainforests where our days had been synchronised with nature – seemed so long ago, so far away. Being still and appreciating the simple things was such a struggle for me in the city. I missed the days where we would spend hours lying on the grass on our big, tie-dyed purple rug, beside a soul-quietening stream or in the shadow of a majestic mountain, serenaded by nothing but the sounds of nature. I missed the peace that was so easy to find there.

While we managed to find some respite in places like Fitzroy Gardens, it seemed like stillness and quietness were scarce commodities indeed. Stopping and smelling the roses is essential. But there are those who love the rush of the city. My friend Elaine thrives in the city, she comes alive with all the lights, the glamour, the noise, the bustle. I guess my point is, whether in the country or the city, it's important to live a balanced life. I am learning that life does NOT start after the bills get paid, the promotion comes through, the kids get sorted, or when we get the new mobile home, or when any other fantasies come true. This is it. Right now. This *is* your life, the very life of life. Learning to live in the moment, and not just for the moment, is a life-changing principal that we need to get a hold of.

* * *

And there's more to what I am learning on this wild journey called *life*. Happiness is a choice; we choose to be happy. Peace is a choice; we choose peace by deciding to live a certain way. Love and respect are a choice regardless of what people may do to us. Thankfulness is a choice, and it never depends on whether we get everything we think we are entitled to or not. Regardless of our circumstances, we can decide to be thankful. Do you know that it is impossible for the seeds of depression to take root in a thankful heart? I am not telling you stuff that I haven't learnt for myself the hard way. There was a time when the seeds of depression not only took root in my heart, but spread through my whole life. I have battled for these choices, and more often than not, the battle wasn't with anyone else except me.

I had to re-tell my story, in my own mind and heart. I had to re-focus my life; or lose it. I had to begin to believe what God says about me, or continue in my dark, weakened state. I am more important to him than anything else in the entire universe, and he is fully committed to me. Because I am loved so much, I don't have to be overly concerned about failing or not measuring up (what release!). I can step out, take whatever risks I need to and be all that I should be. Setbacks don't trip me up and conquer me... they're speed-humps along life's road that I can slow down and manoeuvre, pressing on toward my prize. I can do it – and I don't have to hide behind anything any longer. I can be the best me, I can be. And you can be the most magnificent you that you can be. Woohoo!

CHAPTER SIX
mountains to climb

Having vision for our lives is important. It might not be that you want to fall down stairs, be hit by cars and leap off balconies like my stuntman son, or to travel around in a Buzz-sized van, but we were all created with unique gifts. We are people of unlimited worth, here for a magnificent purpose. We are meant to rise; to have a purpose and a plan.

Hmm, I seem to recall God telling us that 'he has a purpose and a plan for our lives'. Yes, it is chapter 29 and verse 11 of Jeremiah. A great verse to memorise and carry around in your heart. It is a beauty to whip out during hard times to remind yourself there's a purpose for you being here. Nobody is an accident. Nobody, absolutely nobody, is on this planet, right now, by accident. There is a divine plan. A perfect plan put together by a good and gracious and loving God, who just happens to love us to bits! And he says his plan for placing us right here on this earth, right now, right where we are, reading this book is 'to prosper you and give you a future and a hope.' He is so cool in the way he orchestrates everything for our good. That day getting blown out to sea in the dingy at Greenpatch could have been my last (as many others could have), but it wasn't, he orchestrated events to ensure it wasn't.

As our youngest son's wedding drew closer, we didn't have all the money we thought we would to help pay for it. Gulp! We were freaking out, just mildly, but trusting that events would be orchestrated so that the funds would somehow be made available to us. A week prior to the wedding, our son and his fiancée travelled down to his sister's place where we were 'camped'. They had decided on the way, to work out exactly how much money was needed to finish paying off everything needed for the big day. When they arrived at my daughter's, they brought mail with them... we keep a post office box for any mail that may arrive while we are on the road, and they had checked it for us on the way through.

Some of my other children and their partners were gathered by the time my son and his fiancée arrived. They walked in with a comprehensive list and the amount of dollars needed to fulfil it. I opened the mail while everyone was chatting and couldn't believe it. I hadn't worked as a journalist for more than 12 months, but there in the mail was a cheque - back-payment for published photographs I had taken previously. Yeah, you are figuring it out yourself now, aren't you... it was the exact amount needed.

We are loved – passionately! We're meant to live purposefully, not just drift along oblivious and unfulfilled. What are you doing to invest in yourself? One effective tool we can use is goal-setting. How will you know if you are achieving your goals if you don't have any? I mean, you could be the most successful, power-filled, amazing goal-achiever on the planet, and because you haven't written anything down to believe for, you don't even know it. Your dreams could all be coming true, except you don't know it because you don't know what they are. Wow!

* * *

'Camped' in our bed-on-wheels, LiteAce aka 'Buzz', alongside the freezing fresh-flowing waters of Jounama Creek in a valley under the breathtaking beauty of the Snowy Mountains, my husband and I woke early one morning and decided to trek to the top of one of the mountains in the range around about us. We were attempting to conquer this particularly huge mountain so we packed our backpacks with some lunch, water and basics, and set out with determined hearts. It was hard going (and I don't write that lightly) and as the summer day got hotter and hotter, and the mountain got steeper and steeper, my resolve began to wane. I could have easily quit but I dared not mention it out loud. I couldn't get the thought of stopping out of my mind and I began to try to convince myself that I didn't care about the stupid mountain anyway. 'I had nothing to prove,' I kept telling myself. 'It was no big deal, we'd given it a pretty good shot, that was the main thing.' I must have voiced some of these thoughts out loud, because my hubby had stopped leading the way and had turned around for one of our familiar 'counselling' sessions. After a good talking to, I agreed to continue. I hated to admit it, but hubby was right, and we simply couldn't, and wouldn't, allow ourselves to think like that. What we had begun, we would finish. Quitting wasn't an option.

Another hour passed and it seemed like we were barely making any progress. Each time we would round a bend in the ridiculously-steep track I kept expecting to see the summit, but to my dismay all I could see was yet another steep incline disappearing into the distance. My ears went funny, my temples were pounding to the rhythm of my overworked heart, my legs were quickly turning to jelly, my face was doing a great impression of a beetroot, and my backpack was glued to my shirt with sweat. I felt like I had used up all my reserves; that I was running on empty and would soon collapse in a sorry heap. That trail was relentless, and as we headed skyward without reprieve, I put my head down and focused on putting one foot in front of the other - that's all I had left. 'Surely Everest couldn't have been much harder than this,' I consoled myself. Just then - as I was losing hope of ever seeing my loved ones again, and with the words of that old hymn 'Nearer My God to Thee' trembling on my lips - I spied the summit and gave a huge sigh of relief.

The view from the top of the mountain where we enjoyed our well-earned lunch was absolutely breathtaking. Of course, it seemed all the better for having 'earned' such a view. My hands were shaking as I attempted to eat my sandwich, my calf muscles were still screaming in protest, and sweat continued to cascade down my back as I waited for the cool breeze at the top to revive me. I was truly wasted, but I felt invincible. I was the Queen of the Castle, on top of the world! The panoramic view was breathtaking, and as we strained to look back at our camp in the distance, we could just make out our tiny bed-on-wheels sitting there as if it was one of those 'mini-micro' toy cars. After all our effort to get to the top we didn't want to leave too soon, so we sat and tried to take in the whole mountain-top experience, feeling empowered and invigorated. We guzzled as much water as we thought sensible and poured more over our red faces and steaming heads, before discussing whether we should attempt to head back via a trail that appeared to go across the neighbouring mountaintop before descending to camp. I protested, and hubby relented, so we headed back the way we had come. I think by the time we got back to Buzz we were both very appreciative that we hadn't taken the other track down, as we still may have been walking the next day.

The descent was nowhere near as difficult as the assent, but as the pressure was transferred to the front of our legs, we spent the next couple of hours trying to stop ourselves slipping and sliding down the steep rocky decline. Our legs quickly turned to jelly again, as they had done before, but fortunately we had our trusty walking sticks to keep us from skidding all the way down the track on our bums. We both experienced a few close calls, turning our ankles and the like, but I was the only one to lose my footing completely, coming down hard on my knee and losing some 'bark' in the process. After resting for a minute or two to allow the pain to subside, and once a generous coating of spit had been applied to the wound, we continued on our way. We were tingling all over from the exertion and from being on unsteady ground for so long, and as there were still a few kilometres or so to our camp we had to go slow to avoid any further accidents – I didn't fancy hubby having to piggyback me home, and I'm pretty sure he wasn't too keen on the idea either.

We eventually made it to the bottom without any more mishaps, and made a bee-line for the crisp, clean waters of the creek, where we quickly peeled off the few bits of clothing we were still wearing and threw ourselves into one of the natural pools that had been carved into the rocky bed. The water was amazing, freezing cold, but so refreshing and so good. We spent a good half hour there regaining our strength, alternately lolling on the rocks and sliding in for another dip. We were still about a kilometre from our camp so we couldn't afford to collapse and surrender to fatigue just yet. We strolled very slowly and very contentedly back to camp. It was early-to-bed that night, and as we lay in Buzz later that evening, we felt tired, yet at the same time, exhilarated. We were proud of our accomplishment and were enjoying the sense of satisfaction it left us with. I was glad I hadn't quit, that my 'coach' hubby had cheered me on.

There's not much in life that compares with setting goals, working hard towards achieving them, persevering through wanting to give-up, and then experiencing the joy and satisfaction of conquering. It may seem a little thing, to climb a relatively pint-sized mountain, but this experience set a precedent for other challenges we've had to face along the road. Now, when the going gets tough, we take a breather and remind ourselves of our purpose, our vision, and our goals, and we put our heads down and do what we have to do to 'reach the summit'.

CHAPTER SEVEN
breakdown

There was a song written many years back that had lyrics like, 'I get knocked down, but I get up again.' I think Chumbawamba sang it but I'm not sure what year it was. Let me tell you, I used to get knocked down easily – it was the getting up again that was the hard part!

Here's a no-brainer... victory isn't achieved by quitting... have you noticed that? It isn't the quitters standing up on blocks at the Olympics and claiming their medals. It isn't the quitters playing in the footy grand finals. VICTORY only belongs to those who keep focused on the GOAL, and who keep on going, even after they've been knocked down. VICTORY belongs to those who understand there is a *process* to get to the PRIZE, who aren't reduced to stopping because of the *trial*, but rise again on their quest for the TREASURE. It takes guts and determination and it takes practice and understanding your purpose.

We can't wimp out every time something doesn't go right... because it's pretty-well guaranteed that there will be times, if not today, then tomorrow or next month or even next year, that somewhere, somehow, along the journey, things will go pear shaped. Things will even get messed up. BUT, there is hope. VICTORY is PROMISED to those who persevere. My youngest daughter's address for a few years was 'Beach Road, Sunshine Bay'. For real! It sounds like the most idyllic situation, doesn't it? But that's not to say the sand from that beach didn't get in our cossies and create a rash sometimes and the sunshine from that bay didn't slip behind a few clouds now and again.

Now, when I feel inclined to quit, I recognise the symptoms and purposefully stop and give myself a good talking to. I ask myself some questions like: Is this worth getting upset over? Is it really that bad? Is this situation irreparable? Is quitting a better option than persevering? What will I gain by NOT quitting? What will it cost me and am I willing to pay that price?

Don't I have it in me to overcome this hurdle? How do I put a positive spin on this situation?

I try to be real and acknowledge some of the crap isn't pleasant, and I may need some time out occasionally to recover or recuperate. But I also ask for eyes to see that tiny strand of hope, that tiny ray of sunshine, that tiny glimmer of light to give me the oomph I need to rise again. I'm not quitting. I am going to run this race. I'm determined to finish. You need to make a commitment to run *your* race. You are the only one who can! And yes, when you run, you will risk falling – the main thing is to get back up again. Being down isn't the problem – staying down is. Another quote goes, 'I'm either up, or I'm getting up, I've learned not to camp in between.'

One of my granddaughters had a super sore on her knee last week and anyone with eyes could see that it troubled her. It would have hurt, there's no doubt about that. I'm not denying the pain. But one thing I noticed that even a two-year-old can fathom, she didn't go to bed and tell her mummy that she was quitting and wouldn't get up until she was all better in a week's time. She took the parental magical kiss of healing, a quick prayer, the miracle-strip commonly known as the bandaid (and if it's fluoro-blue it carries extra healing powers), and voila, she was up again. She took mummy's hand and began to walk again. Five minutes later, she was running.

If you are one who has given up because you have tried and tried again yet it seems to be to no avail; allow me to suggest you give your frustration to God right now. Seeing instant results to prayer sure can be a faith-builder, and who doesn't need those! But God isn't some fantasy santa who we send a list of wants to so that he can wave a magic wand and grant our wishes (otherwise I'd be driving a you-beaut flashy mobile-home by now instead of living in a bed-on-wheels). Sometimes God delivers instantly and says, 'yes!' Sometimes he says, 'wait.' And other times he says, 'no'. Yeah, that's right, NO is a Godly answer. If you are a 'yes'-person who goes around agreeing to every task anyone asks of you, you need to know that NO is OK. Just think, if God said 'yes' to everything we wanted, the world would be absolute chaos in no time. God, as any good father should, is protecting us from ourselves when he gives us a 'no'. If it is not good for you or for others, NO is the ONLY answer.

I used to be a 'yes'-person. I was easily manipulated. I only needed someone to tell me I would be good at something and I would feel obliged to do it, whether I wanted to or not. I would do it to people-please most of the time, which usually indicates a self-esteem issue. I was attempting to override my low self-esteem through the accolades I hoped to get from others.

One person asked me to help run a youth group, and I said yes. Another asked me to head-up a branch of their local service club, and I said yes. Another asked me to organise a lunchtime group in our local high school, and I said yes. Yet another thought I would be a great wedding photographer for a friend of theirs, and I said yes. I was saying yes to every suggestion that came my way. My schedule was jam packed. I was such a high achiever... hmm, or was I? It turns out I wasn't really called to do any of those things. Sure I was busy, but I wasn't fulfilling my life's purpose. I was running around like a chook with its head cut off!

I wasn't really passionate about any of those things because they weren't part of my purpose. There wasn't anything wrong with any of those tasks; they just hadn't been planted in my heart for me to fulfil. I was so busy doing what everyone else wanted me to do, I had no time to do what I wanted to do - or to be myself. If I had focused my energies on doing one thing well, it may have been more fruitful. But even so, I needed to take the time out to find myself again and refocus on what I needed to make a priority. At the time of all this senseless busyness I was employed part-time and had my children to care for. I was flat out, flat chat and burning out! So, what did I do?

I had an emotional breakdown. I opted to get off the merry-go-round.

Obviously at the time I didn't just stop and make a conscious decision to break down. I broke down. It might sound weird for me to say, but in hindsight my breakdown served a valuable purpose by making me stop and reassess my whole life. I opted out of all my responsibilities (because I couldn't cope with any of them) and I had time – time to sit, time to think. I'd reached the end of my road, a dead end, and I couldn't find my way back out.

I can see now, had I exercised some wisdom along the way, I wouldn't have 'needed' to break down to escape life; I could simply have made a few wise decisions. But I wasn't thinking rationally because I had a lot of soul issues that were driving me to do all this stuff. I was looking for value and worth in what I did, rather than who I was. Maybe if I would have been living MY life, doing the things I felt called to do and equipped to do, I could have escaped the breakdown. But I wasn't and I didn't.

Struggling with my own sense of unworthiness drove me to work harder to please more people, but it never improved my self-worth. No matter how many times I said 'yes' the negativity inside me never diminished. The problem was at the foundation of my life, all the other things I'd built needed to be stripped back so I could work on my foundations. I could liken it to trying to build a tree house at the top of a rotted-out tree. No matter how great the tree house is, it will crumble when the dead tree crumbles.

It was a traumatic time in my life. One that I'm determined never to repeat. It hurt. It hurt bad. I had become so weak from my heavy load that I could no longer keep my job. I became so tired I could no longer fulfil the evening commitments I'd said 'yes' to. I became so exhausted I could no longer cope with the noise of our happy children in our home. I couldn't sleep, but I was so tired. I couldn't concentrate or even think straight. I felt good for nothing. I quit everything. EVERYTHING. I left my volunteer work, my paid employment, my groups and, unfortunately, my family.

Because of my own neediness I allowed myself to be manipulated - there's a lot of opportunistic people out there who know how to push your buttons to get you to do what they want you to do. Those people I thought were my friends and greatest supporters were nowhere to be seen when I had my breakdown. I'd worked so hard to gain their approval and now some saw me as a useless failure. I had gotten it so wrong. Self-worth was never meant to be derived from what we do, what we achieve, or what others think of us. If I'd known what I know now, I could have saved myself, my family and friends a whole lot of trouble and heartache. I still carry some pain over what I put my loving family through at that time - don't get me wrong, I know I have forgiveness, and I have forgiven myself for all that happened - but talking about it still makes my heart ache.

I had almost been ready to quit. Quit everything. And I don't just mean the jobs, volunteer work and my beautiful family. I mean life. That is a very dangerous place to be. In the first 20 years of my life suicidal-thoughts and tendencies, self-harming plans and plotting were very real to me. There I was, almost 20 years on, and it was like I'd gone all the way around a mountain only to come back to the very same spot! Obviously there were some important lessons for me to learn. I could learn them during my time of solitude and self-imposed exile, or I could go round that same mountain again. I needed to face some realities about myself, my personality, my dreams and my future, and I needed to make different choices than I had been making. I had read about the Israelites wandering in the desert for 40 years before they could enter their promised land, and I was praying like crazy that it wasn't going to take me another 20 years to get where God was trying to lead me. I needed to listen, and I needed to listen good. I needed to trust. I needed to believe. I needed the reality of God's plan just for me to sink in. I needed God's love and grace to heal my wounded soul. I was saved, I was sure of that – yet I wasn't completely free. In John chapter eight the bible says, 'So if the Son sets you free, you are truly free', so what had happened to me? I had allowed his love and light into my life but had kept him out of some areas for fear of what he might think or what he might want to change. I can liken it to inviting a guest into my lounge room but I wouldn't dare let them see the mess in the spare room.

And so began my quest for wellness. From memory, I was in my zombie-like state for a couple of months before I could rise and begin to think of the day ahead of me. So it took a little longer before I could think about the future at all. I allowed myself time. Time I had. I sought counselling and allowed myself to hurt and to heal - at my own pace. I learnt heaps of stuff during that time, about myself and life in general. I learnt to relax. Relaxing actually became kind of fun. I rekindled my appreciation of nature (inherited from my dad). I lived near an inlet at the time, and would spend hours down there, watching the birdlife and the soldier crabs, the sunrises and the changing tides. It was a time of beauty in the ashes for me. I started to enjoy my own company and revel in the silence - going against the grain of my sanguine nature - so it was a real learning curve. I HAD to learn to be alone, because I had heart palpitations and anxiety if I was around more than a couple of people! I wasn't ready to re-enter society for a long time, maybe six to eight months, but as I look back now, I became a new person during my time of hibernation. I guess I was like a caterpillar crawling around the earth, until I slipped into my cocoon for the transformation process to take place, eventually emerging as a beautiful butterfly. To cut a long and difficult story short, that was what it was like for me. I grew wings. There's a quote a friend of mine shared with me recently, 'When you find yourself cocooned in isolation and despair and cannot find your way to the light, remember, this is the place where caterpillars go, in order to grow their wings.'

During that time I began to try and find myself, my real self, to uncover and bring to light the person God said I was. Using the bible, I compiled a list of the good things he said about me: I am a jewel in his crown, the apple of his eye. His treasure, his bride, his daughter and his most precious possession. 'You are precious to me, you are honoured and I love you,' he says through the prophet Isaiah (43:4). I began to realise my strength came from who HE SAID I WAS, not from who I THOUGHT I WAS. I began to grow in my understanding of his grace. It wasn't what I could do that pleased God, but who I was. My being excited him, not necessarily my doing. He had created me a human being, not a human doing, and through that revelation my healing and restoration accelerated dramatically. When the little light within me finally switched on, I realised that my fear of rejection had driven me to focus my energies on all I could do, instead of relaxing and working on all I could be!

Everything takes time - time to heal and time to rebuild. I set small challenges for myself and joined some 12-step programs to be with like-minded people, people who wanted to get real. I continued counselling. I tested my wings – my way, in my time and I became a 'no' person. I actually had little secret giggles to myself whenever anyone asked me to do something. My immediate reaction would be 'no' and I wouldn't even explain myself. If I didn't want to do something, that was good enough for me. I wasn't being selfish, far from it, I was finally being sensible. During my recovery journey I spent time with friends and re-bonded with my amazing family. I even visited extended family and renewed my connection with them. I became more confident and independent. By the end of an agonising yet incredibly rewarding 12 months, I had completely re-united with my family. (God bless them all for their patience!)

I'd like to mention here that my hubby and I had decided to renew our wedding vows a few years prior to my breakdown, not because we had to, but because we wanted to reaffirm our decision to be together for the rest of our lives. We had started our relationship together as teenagers, and after I had discovered I was pregnant, we decided to 'do the right thing' and get married. We realised we had much more choice in the matter. We could stay together because we wanted to, or we could go our own separate ways. The renewing of our vows was a glorious celebration of healing and the strength of family ties, with all of our five children involved in the wedding party. Even as I type this, tears pour out automatically. With this renewing so strong within my mind throughout those dark days, words cannot express some of my thoughts and feelings, neither can they express my sense of jubilation, victory and relief as restoration gently unfolded within my life and marriage again. I was beginning again, again. I began to see God's hand of grace in the bright, radiant sunshine of my restoration. Without my breakdown I may never have learnt who I really am and what I was made for, and even worse, I may have missed out on the privilege of drawing closer to my creator and experiencing his amazing love and grace. I was knocked down, way down, but I now walk upright - chin up, chest out, shoulders back - proud to be alive!

CHAPTER EIGHT
post-it notes

As I write this, I have a super-cute granddaughter on my knee. I know you know that all babies are cute, but she is more than cute to me, she is extra special. We've got a precious bond. My bloodline courses through her veins. She's my baby's baby! I held her mummy in my arms all those years ago and the circle of life continues. I want to get to really know her as she grows, and I want her to really know me. We're connected forever; we're family. She's one of my rich treasures. My heart lights up when I see her. All her achievements - 'she can wave'; 'she said 'ta'' - thrill me. I want to be actively involved in her life, watching out for her, protecting her, encouraging her, loving her. God's like that with us, only more so. If you magnified my love, multiplied it, then added some more, you'd be getting close to God's love for us! He LOVES and DELIGHTS in us. You know he looked down on my first steps and was pointing me out proudly to his angels saying, 'That's my girl!' It's a mind-blowing concept, but he was there when I spoke my first words, and he'll be there for my last. He loves, protects, provides, plans for, and delights over us. Knowing that we are loved like this gives us the confidence to be ourselves and provides a huge step-up for living a healthier, happier life.

Our eldest son worked in real estate for a few years and he tells the story of a farmer who decided to sell his property. My son went out to see the land, had the farmer describe the property, and snapped some photos. He put an advertising promo together and sought the permission of the farmer to use it. When the farmer saw what my son had put together his response was, 'I don't want to sell it, I've been looking for something like this my whole life!'

It isn't happiness that makes us grateful, but gratefulness that makes us happy. That guy had what he'd always wanted, he just hadn't stopped to realise it. One of my sayings, of the zillions that I collect from all over the place, says, 'If you can't be grateful for what you receive, be grateful for what you escape.' It does me good to recognise all the positive things I have in my life, and to be grateful for the negative stuff I haven't had to deal with. There are those who don't quite know what they want, but they are sure they don't have it. It may take a lot of discipline and effort to turn the 'glass is half empty' perspective, into the more desirable, 'glass is half full' attitude, but believe me, it's worth it. Instead of whinging and complaining about what we haven't got, take a lesson from our farmer friend and try to 'see' what we already have, and be thankful for it. There really is no other way to become a genuinely contented person.

Because I now understand the implications of gratefulness in relation to life-quality, emotional stability, and attaining goals, I often include the concept when I'm public speaking. We need to love who we are, and be grateful right where we are, because if we can't find satisfaction in what we have now, we'll be hard-pressed to find it even if we get what we want or think we need.

Results from numerous studies confirm that a positive, thankful attitude has many desirable outcomes. Some benefits include: improved moods, better coping behaviours, stronger relationships, greater resistance to disease, higher self-esteem, and an overall sense that all is ok with the universe. Wow, think about it, that's proven benefits mentally, emotionally, physically, psychologically and spiritually – Woohoo! Though I wasn't personally interviewed for any of these studies, I've been on both sides of the track and can vouch for the results. I used to be someone who thought I always needed 'just one more thing' to be happy. You probably know some people like that. 'If there was just a little more money' or 'if only I had a better job' or 'maybe if I move house again'. You know the stories. But it has been proven time and again, those who aren't grateful for what they have, couldn't even find happiness if what they had was doubled. Don't fall into the trap of waiting for the 'something else' to come along before you give yourself permission to enjoy life.

And it's not just about whether you are an optimist or a pessimist... I think I began as a pessimist, switched to optimism and advanced to 'my glass is full and running over!' For me it's now the only way to see things. The bible says in Luke 6:38, 'Give and you will receive. Your gift will return to you in full – pressed down, shaken together to make room for more, running over, and poured into your lap.' It goes on to say, 'The measure you give will be the measure you get back.' Not only am I to be grateful, but I'm to gratefully give. By living a life like that, we get to reap all the soulful benefits that come with being a giver ('It is more blessed to give than it is to receive'), and we can confidently expect to have our material needs taken care of because 'as you sow, so shall you reap.'

I've been a slow learner, but more and more I am learning the value and power of thankfulness. It's through gratitude that I've gained inspiration to live well and to grow further. It's through giving that I've opened my life to receive. I sow, I reap. I plant, I harvest. My knowledge of God's love compels me to EXPECT him to provide for me so I can then provide for others. I expect him to answer my prayers, forgive me, watch over me and help me dream and fulfil my purpose. His blood is coursing through my veins, just like my blood has continued through my little granddaughter who is jiggling on my knee as I struggle to keep her fingers from my keyboard. I've got his DNA!

Even in setting goals for our own lives, let's allow love and gratefulness to be our motivation. God expects us to genuinely love others, not just say we love them when we really don't. In all our ambitions, let's ensure genuine love shines through. How could we NOT be happy living a life like that?

I live a fairly balanced life... now - a far cry from my messy past (you're bound to hear more about that as we go along). From a lonely self-loathing 'victim', I'm now surrounded by truck-loads of amazing, incredibly-loving people. Without their contribution, without their love and patience, I wouldn't be half the person I am today (throughout the book I'll introduce some of them so you can understand the wealth they bring to my life). I don't believe there are any self-made people. But even if I'm wrong and there are, they must be pretty bored when they get to the top, crack open that bottle of natural sparkling mineral water (my preferred bubbly) and have nobody there to clink glasses with.

Today, hubby and I have an eclectic bunch - we have children in the city and the country; children who rent apartments and children who own homes. We have children working as professionals or tradespeople, and those who've chosen full-time motherhood. We have a fireman, a stuntman, musicians and songwriters, an optical dispenser, a minister, a circus instructor (or circus freak as we lovingly refer to him), and a fencer (touché). Two own their own business, one runs a gym, one serves in a cafe, one is in the Australian Forces, and another is head graphic designer in a big city church – and yet their parents (that's me and hubby) thrive in a tiny van!

As you can see, I'm surrounded by interesting people. There is my delightful husband, whom I adore, sometimes much, and sometimes decidedly less, throughout our rocky, tumultuous marriage. I could have pretended that we have been on a continuous journey of romantic bliss together, but we haven't. It's that kind of bullshit that causes couples to think they are doing something wrong, simply because they had a fight, or two. Come on! Get real! I have listened to older couples who dare not mention the mess involved along the journey – as if mess equals weakness or sin. Well friends, be released from that wrong mindset right now and breathe a sigh of relief. Marriage is a kaleidoscopic, rainbow-coloured, cloudy, sunny, hot, cold, incredibly wild roller-coaster ride. Just hold on, keep screaming and laughing alternately together and enjoy it. During my years of denial and our years of drug and alcohol addictions, we couldn't be open, frank or objective about ourselves or our relationship, and that was incredibly hard work to maintain. Yes, there is pain and joy. All of it is easier if you SUPPORT one another through it, and don't pull apart and play the blame-game.

I have to tell you though, that there was a particular period of time in our marriage when I could not bear to look at Step. Normally his handsome face makes my heart skip a beat. But one day I arrived home to the stark reality that I could not look at his face, not without grimacing. I guess his curly locks which were '70s afro-style when I met him, and have varied in length and style with each changing era - now more like wild Bob Marley dreadlocks - must frame his face in such a way as to bring out the best of his features. This day, on a stinking hot heat-wave in January, I arrived home to be greeted by a beanie-wearing, wildly-grinning weirdo, complete with beady eyes sparkling in a demented kind of way. He whisked the beanie off to reveal a large, round, white, TOTALLY BALD, giant-sized head. 'What the?' I gasped, taking a step backwards. I mean, I knew his head was big. It is like a melon on a toothpick! We have to buy extra-large pillows and sew two together for him to sleep at night. But his dark curly locks normally contained it in a bearably cute kind of way. The locks were gone. His melon was as white as a giant baby's bum.

Sitting so I didn't have to look at him, he told me the tragic tale. For some reason that morning his curls had seemed more unruly than ever, so out came the clippers for a quick trim. Running over his head with a 'number four' comb usually did the trick, but oh no, not this time. Next came the 'just been released from prison' look as he guided a 'number one' comb over his foolish head. Finally, with all restraint gone, he lathered up his obviously empty head, picked up his razor and... the rest is history. Oh the crazy, impulsive things we do.

Once my initial shock wore off, we sat and laughed together, shaking our heads; my stunned one and his huge, fluorescent-white one. The good news was he was able to wear a cap throughout the rest of summer, keeping it hidden from others. The bad news was I couldn't bear to sleep beside a creepy hairless man, so I made him wear a beanie to bed every night. And even though he sweated like crazy, he wore that thing every night until he looked like my hubby again. Whenever we think about that episode it still cracks us up.

The marriage hasn't been a bed of roses, unless you include the thorns. Hmm, maybe a bed of rose bushes... the soft, sweet-scented petals and the prickly, painful thorns all in the one double bed. Though I did hear a saying that goes like this, 'Some complain that the rose has thorns, others rejoice that the thorns have roses.' There's that balance and reality again – and the marriage-saving wonder of a simple beanie. Anyway, as you know, there is my doting husband, with a love language of service, so I've got it really good there. My love language is words of affirmation and touch, so he also has it really good. All the other stuff we battle out between us. One of his really attractive attributes is that he is constantly thinking of others. He meets people's needs even before they've realised they have a need. He gives. He serves. That's his thing. That's what he brings to the table. The goodness in me has been nurtured, patiently and tender-heartedly, by this incredible man.

Step is a gifted teacher, and has a memory of bionic proportions and an unquenchable thirst for knowledge. He has a heart to see people made whole and live up to their potential. I am very blessed to have him beside me. He believes in my dreams as a writer and an inspirational speaker. Together, we make a good team and often have the joy of seeing people set free and empowered to live the life they were made to live. It is an exciting journey... we have soooo much more to achieve, and look forward to the challenge.

After I delivered our first-born, hubby bought me an eternity ring. It fits snugly next to my engagement ring (the one with the cubic zirconia that was bought on sale, in a rush, whilst shopping for our wedding rings after we discovered the pregnancy of said first son. Oh, and for those that don't know, a cubic zirconia is a low cost, synthetic 'stone' with a visual likeness to the more traditional engagement stone, the expensive diamond). When this son was about five-years-old, he asked me what the eternity ring meant. I told him that his daddy had given it to me after his birth, as a sign that 'mummy and daddy would be together forever.' He looked at me, a tad bewildered, 'Daddy can't be with you forever,' he stated matter-of-factly. Naturally I asked him why not, and he told me, 'Because Daddy has to go to work sometimes.'

Back to my men... there are my two big brothers, who I gave hell to when we were growing up together, yet who adore me and would do anything for me. One phone call and they are here for me. Then add my two sons, my amazing men-children who are not ashamed to hug their mum, or their dad. Yes, even in public! These guys are super heroes, to me. They add so much strength to our family. They are so uniquely different; an essential part of the 'whole'. They are trustworthy men. Our eldest has always taken his role as number one son seriously and is constantly on the look-out for his siblings, as it's his nature to nurture and provide, even though they are all grown up with families of their own. He carries the weight of responsibility as most eldest children do, loving his family in his own special way, and we appreciate that. He has set a high bar, and we are always encouraged to rise. He has always been a helpful person, which he gets from his dad, and one day when he was about nine-years-old and his little bro was four, he had done so much for his siblings that his little brother was impressed enough to come and share his admiration. He looked up at me, gleaming, and said, 'Mummy isn't my big brother a handsome boy?' He meant 'helpful', but he is right, he is handsome too.

He is an entrepreneur. From about the age of nine he's shown signs of having good business sense. Remember the farm where chooks ran around with their heads cut off? Well, at his request, we bought him half a dozen chooks. From then on everything was his responsibility. He would gather the eggs and sell them to the health food store, using the profits to buy the feed he needed to keep his little business running. He was very diligent and faithful with the egg business, and after some additional work at a supermarket a few years later, bought himself his first sound system – and my hubby was green with envy because it kicked-butt over his crappy, old one.

My youngest son, as you already know, is a nut-case. Just yesterday he was 'getting hit over the head with a crowbar' in his first short film as a stuntman. Fortunately, the crowbar was made of rubber, but don't let on I told you so. From the moment he swung down off that umbilical cord he has been so confident to be himself. He wears his heart on his sleeve and stands for truth and justice, like a caped crusader.

This youngest son of ours purchased his first condom at the age of eight. One day, as I was sorting through the clothes to be washed, I found a condom in the pocket of his jeans. I have to admit I was more than a little taken aback by my discovery, so I confronted him for an explanation. I showed him the little packet from his jeans pocket, and asked him if he knew what it was. With a cheeky grin on his face - the same cheeky grin he wears to this day - he nodded. The plot thickened when I asked him where he got it from and he told me he got it 'at church'. You see, the church we had been attending held their Sunday service in the auditorium of the local golf club. Each week we gave the children something to put in the offering, and this particular day we had given our son $2. Prior to the offering being collected though, he had gone to the toilet and had been intrigued by the condom-vending machine and simply couldn't resist. Once the details were out, I asked him if he knew what it was for and he nodded, again with the cheeky grin. I went on to suggest that he probably wouldn't be in need of it for quite some time, so I would hold onto it for him. He agreed that was a good idea and happily went off to play with his siblings.

Now add to that mix my three sons-in-law, who I insist on calling my 'sons-in-love', which totally creeps them out. These guys sure add some flavour and spice to the family cooking pot. They each are the perfect match for my daughters, and I love them to the moon and back. They have brought with them surfboards, kayaks and jet skis, fishing rods, motorbikes, utes and circus tricks, along with wisdom, leadership and love. I consider them family and friends - strong, deliberate, fun-loving healthy men. Then there is our surrogate son, who stumbled into our lives, and my heart, as a 12-year-old, about 14 years ago, who is a father now with two sons of his own. He's what you might call a rough diamond and he tends to balance out the mix. He currently lives in a tent, and it's not because he necessarily has to but because he chooses to. He calls it the 'Taj'. Yeah, I guess with 'parents' like us, he figured he could go one better than living in a van ha-ha. If we are getting too stuffy or serious about life, I get a Joel fix. He is so real and honest without any pretence. I adore him.

My dad (my hero and mentor), who passed away almost ten years back, used to say to me when I was little, 'Never let the sun go down on your anger.' He wouldn't allow family rifts to continue to the next day, everyone had to 'kiss and make up' by bed time. I really respect that kind of upbringing, and we have attempted to thread it through the tapestry of our family, and believe our kids are doing the same. This principle dad taught comes from the bible in Ephesians 4:26, 'Don't let the sun go down while you are still angry for anger gives a foothold to the devil.'

* * *

I am being completely honest with you when I say there would be no me, and therefore no happy family for me to write about had I not taken stock of my life and made some changes. I respect that some readers may be struggling to find things to be thankful for, but I urge you to start small. Be thankful for some little thing in your life and go from there. Make a list if you need to. Maybe ask a friend to help you to see and appreciate all you have. Be grateful and thankful, and if needed, use visual reminders. Sometimes post-it notes on your mirror will do it.

My youngest son, the stuntman (I love saying that), had a period of time where his injuries had him bedridden. He was medically diagnosed with a spinal disorder and advised to give up his 'stunting' – is that a word? By now, you already know the passion and enthusiasm of this guy. I mean there isn't a negative bone in his beaten-up body. His self-talk is switched on and secure. He dragged his weary, broken body to another professional. This professional agreed with the diagnosis of the disorder, but believed that with treatment, exercise and conscious effort the condition would improve. My son had to concentrate on his posture at all times. He could not get slack about this. He had post-it notes on his bathroom mirror, on the rear-vision mirror of his car, on his steering wheel, in his workbag, on his mobile phone, beside his bed – I mean EVERYWHERE. Now it's automatic. He stands erect, he checks his posture when he is sitting down and he's conscious of how he lifts things (and how he falls). He is fully aware of his body and is in tune to its warning signals when he is getting fatigued. He has successfully re-trained his brain and body, but I'm sure you will still find the odd post-it note or two around about him, to remind him to be vigilant.

Become aware of your inner dialogue, change your self-talk if you need to, and you can re-train your thinking. I was caught-up in negative thinking all day, and living on a permanent downer. I missed all that was beautiful and amazing around me. In order to break patterns of negativity, worry and fear, I first had to become aware of those patterns. Awareness always precedes change. I thought about who I was spending most of my time with, and began building a network of positive people around me. I made a decision to hang out with uplifting people. Are you positioned for the change you need in your life right now? It may take post-it notes stuck all over your face, but you can do it. And whatever you do, don't forget to count your blessings and be thankful.

Grab your post-it notes now and start writing positives about yourself. Plaster them around your home and car where you will actually see them. Add more and more as you get the hang of it. Then keep reading these words and phrases and speak them out loud until it sinks into your brain and you actually believe them.

CHAPTER NINE
break-away bunnies

Not only am I surrounded by great guys, I am also surrounded by positive, encouraging gals - my mother, sister, my three daughters and my daughter-in-love (she handles the title more graciously than my men do). Mum and I rarely saw eye-to-eye on ANYTHING for many, many years, but now we've become best friends.

No matter how old your youngest child is, they remain 'the baby'. Our youngest daughter, 'the baby', now mother of two with another on the way, is a self-sacrificing soul who looks for the good in everyone, and because of her tender heart, is disturbed by discord. She knows the human heart, and taps into it mystically and magically; composing songs that move people to tears... our tender-hearted lioness! Her acoustic performances are spellbinding.

She is a lover of life and a lover of animals. From mice and fish to kittens and rabbits – the number and variety of pets continues to grow. Recently she and her little family went on a holiday. Step and I were the nominated 'animal-sitters' at their cottage in the woods. It was winter time with days of torrential rain, so we moved a mattress onto their lounge room floor in front of the warm fire for the week. It seemed a simple enough task – feed the menagerie of animals; surely even a child could do it. Unfortunately for us, the four rabbits had just been transferred into a new cage the day before our daughter and her family left – it was the Taj Mahal of cages I might add. This you-beaut, state-of-the-art rabbit hutch had two levels, with doors and hinges everywhere, even carpet on the roof. About the only thing it didn't have was wire on the bottom of the cage. Now, I don't know about you, but I would presume wire on the bottom of a rabbit cage would be a fairly essential detail, considering they are naturally burrowing creatures. But, no, this hutch-of-all-hutches was floorless (not flawless); and on the first night of our watch, all four bunnies dug their way out, under the frame of the hutch and disappeared into the bush surrounding the house. Acres and acres of bush – possibly housing dozens of hungry foxes who would kill (literally) for a juicy fresh rabbit. Catching bunnies is not an easy task – believe me, we tried for two days and nights!

You may or may not believe in the power of prayer, but there comes a time in most lives where we resort to prayer whether we believe or not. Personally, I know the power of prayer and so I asked God to do a miracle and bring back the bunnies. Please! One by one, those bunnies came back to the Taj Mahal as though it were Noah's Ark and the world were about to flood. It was incredible. Within 36 hours, all four rabbits had returned safely home. And we were clever enough to put them into the old, broken-down hutch with the wire bottom. I sent my daughter a text about their dodgy new cage AFTER God had miraculously returned the bunnies from the bush.

Though it was a long 36 hours wait til those bunnies returned to the 'ark'; God is never late. He's always on time. We might think it could have, or should have, been done sooner, but his timing is just right. And his timing in bringing this daughter, our baby, into the world was impeccable. Hubby, who was working full-time and studying in his 'spare time', had suggested we not have any more children until his studies were complete. It seemed like a brilliant plan – if only we had managed to stick to it. No sooner than making our decision, we discovered we were 'with child'. At that time we had two boys and two girls – a neat little family, and suddenly we were about to have another child. Amidst the home-schooling, the farm chores (which included chopping wood, milking goats, tending the enormous vegie patch and feeding our own menagerie of animals at that time), Step's studies and full-time work, we were about to add another child to the mix. We knew we would cope but were still a little nervous about how it would all pan out.

From the day she was born, our family seemed complete. The older siblings adored her, and our youngest son bonded to her like a Siamese twin. Life was wonderful. It's funny how we can think we know what's best for us, and then suddenly something comes along to rock our world and it turns out to be just what we needed. Our baby daughter turned out to be a little bundle of joy for the whole family, a gift straight from heaven. We sure were thankful God was calling the shots, not us.

When she was little, she used to bring us such laughter through some of her innocent funny sayings. One time, after she had been sitting on her feet while watching television, she went to get up and announced, 'I can't walk, my feet are all dizzy.' She also used to think pedestrian crossings were called 'desperate' crossings. To this day we still call them that. Some things just stick.

Nobody impersonates comedian Magda Szubanski like my eldest daughter, who keeps us in stitches with her outbreaks of spontaneous impersonations. Though this daughter is more level-headed than her parents, and has wisdom beyond her years, she is a regular comedian. A couple of her more hilarious renditions include Alfalfa's love letter to Darla from the Little Rascals movie, and Rowan Atkinson's 'Whistler's Mother's speech' from the Bean movie – both of which she performed at her recent 30th birthday celebrations, where all guests were required to wear zany wigs. She is such a clown, and once she gets on a roll there's no stopping her. Her husband, the minister, just sits there and laughs his head off at her silly antics, knowing that he has no chance of pulling her up. During her school days she even started-up her own drama group that met and practised during lunch breaks. She was so popular amongst the kids at school that they voted her the sport House Captain - the irony is she never actually participated in sport at all, but she did cheer and yell the loudest for those who did. Her passion for family and children has no equal. She was born to be a mum and has done a great job with two of our adorable granddaughters. She is a tireless encourager of young mums, runs the Sunday-school program at church, and teaches Scripture in the local primary school. She has a gift for gathering children not unlike the Pied Piper.

Every family needs a princess, and our middle daughter definitely fits the bill. For years, when asked what she wanted to be when she grew up, her answer was, 'I'm going to be a fairy princess.' And to this day she is the one in the family most likely to spend more of her hard-earned pay on new clothes and constantly-changing hairdos. Being a great encourager and a faithful friend, she is invariably surrounded by people. Just as our eldest daughter gathers children, so this daughter gathers people - of all ages and backgrounds. She is the reason the term 'people-person' was invented. She is the life of the party, yet sensitive and in tune to what others are going through. She has a passion for the underdog and is always ready to lend a helping hand to those who are struggling. Living and working in the city, she is our shopper, our manic consumer. Clothes, shoes, makeup, and accessories are her Achilles heel, but in spite of that she remains a very generous soul. Her most recent claim to fame is delivering our first grandson. She is also our world-traveller, spending years exploring, living and working overseas, while hubby and I lived vicariously through her adventures. At the rate we are going with our travels, it may take us the next 20 years just to explore Australia.

Daughter-in-love is a delight... an outstanding photographer and talented designer. Different from our 'blood' girls, but a true sister to them. She loves family. She is one of those arty types that dresses creatively, thinks so far outside the box that she invents her own, floats through life with flowers in her hair and beads dangling from her elegant neck, and sees beauty in everything. She is a gracious person with a soft and sensitive heart, so much so that even our friendly bantering can sometimes cause her concern that someone may get hurt. Of course, when you grow up in a family like ours, you get used to being stirred about your peculiarities, but it's all done in a light-hearted way, and it does serve to strengthen family ties. Nothing is allowed to go so far as to hurt anyone though, and everyone knows the spirit with which the 'razzing' is delivered.

Last, but not least, is my little sister. We hated each other's stinking guts (in the nicest, sibling-rivalry-driven way), throughout our tumultuous early years living together in the same house, sharing the same pokey little bedroom (and unfortunately, sharing the same distressing sexual-assault experience at the hands of a stranger). Once we began to pop out our kiddies though, a day barely passed without us seeing one another. We did tennis and mothers' group together; we shopped, picnicked, swam, relaxed, and generally did life together - just like my daughters are doing now. She currently lives in another state of Oz, is a busy career-woman, and like myself, is a proud grandmother. Over the years our roles have alternated, where sometimes I'm her protector, and at other times she is mine. In spite of all we've been through we have the utmost love and respect for one another, and like most strong women, our sibling rivalry continues.

Perhaps one of the reasons I'm passionate about families is that wherever we go - on our travels or just doing everyday life - we meet so many kids who are from broken families. Sadly, it seems that the family unit as I know it, and as my children and grandchildren know it, is a rare and endangered species today. It's a shame that we don't seem to comprehend just how important 'family' is to the on-going health and wellbeing of our communities, and our culture as a whole. Healthy families are the essential bricks-and-mortar of a community, and I believe it is up to each one of us to esteem and uphold the sacredness of family so that it isn't lost to future generations. If you would like to be part of a great family, for your own sake, and for the sake of your children, then I suggest you take up the challenge and be the one to make the difference in your family situation. Jesus said, 'Blessed are the peace-makers, for they shall be called children of God'. You can take the initiative and be the one to forgive first and let go of any grudges, hurts and resentments that may be festering within the family and causing disunity. Be the mature one, the 'big' person who forgives, rather than the immature, 'little' person who hangs on to every offense. If you do these things, your personal life and your family life will change for the better – guaranteed (God's guarantee, not mine)! Make the decision now, set the example, take the initiative - you can bring healing and restoration to your family, you can be like glue, holding it together when times are tough.

Recently, one of my granddaughters was learning to ride her bike without training wheels. Her daddy and one of her uncles were there to give the necessary encouragement she needed to succeed. They had explained all the methods and techniques to her, and even mummy had coached her some. But the only way she learnt to ride that bike without training wheels, was to get on and start peddling. She was pretty shaky to start with but after a while she got the hang of it and wondered why she hadn't tried it sooner. So, if you really want a better family and a better community to live in, get on your bike, start pedalling (even if it is all wobbly to start with), have faith in yourself and in God's promises, and keep at it until it becomes second nature.

CHAPTER TEN
blooming flowers

During the time of my emotional breakdown, I began to truly appreciate the tranquillity of gardens. I like the growth, the beauty, the butterflies and the prolific range of colours found within gardens. I love seeing things blossom. That's what we're meant to do here in God's garden, blossom where we're planted.

I remember a glorious garden experience while camped beside a river in a National Park, a couple of hours inland from the central coast area of NSW. We were fortunate to experience the place during some unusually sunny days through late autumn. Enticed by the beauty of the place, we decided to set up camp for the night. Step was preparing what had originally been our lunch meal, but because life on the road can be so willy-nilly, it ended up being our evening meal instead. While I was making myself comfortable on my purple and green fluffy cushions beside the fire, writing about the days' events, hubby was cooking us up a treat (most people can't believe the gourmet meals he miraculously whips-up around the camp-fire). Anyway, by this time we had Buzz all snuggly 'tarped-up' in case of rain, and to keep us extra warm of a night (we had learnt to prepare for variable weather conditions no matter how sunny it seemed). It had only taken us about fifteen minutes to gather our wood, saw it up and have it ready beside the fire that hubby was creating a culinary delight upon. We had learnt a lot of shortcuts in setting-up camp by this stage in our travels, so turning our surroundings into 'home' was now accomplished quickly and efficiently – like a well-oiled machine.

On that particular day we had no mobile reception… we had lost service hours previously as we travelled down the winding, narrow road to our destination. Having little or no way to communicate with the outside world had become a common occurrence and I was beginning to enjoy, rather than panic over, the solitude and sense of isolation. The river beside us was gurgling playfully, and its waters were clear, fresh and FREEZING cold. We had food and water, light and warmth, and were bathed in beauty - all the simple luxuries of life. I remember stopping and sitting still to listen to and soak in the scene with its plush carpet of leaves - some still gently falling, and the curling and swirling of the camp-fire smoke. It seemed the whole of nature spoke of order and purpose - the design of a loving master gardener. Haunting ghost-gums and craggy, old spotted-gums provided a natural canopy, as the light through their branches dappled everything around about. From our snug camp site, with the warmth of the afternoon sun quickly fading, I marvelled at the small birds flitting and twittering around us, the clear yellow eyes of the nosey, black currawongs, kookaburras with their imposing beaks and manic laughter, and the vibrant crimson breasts of the rosellas perched cautiously close by. Exposed tree roots littered the ground like discarded kangaroo tails, and abandoned, rock-ringed fireplaces - prospective campsites of tomorrow - completed the enchanting scene. As an overwhelming sense of peace and the wonder of creation gently washed over me, I felt at home.

There's a quirky saying I want to share with you, 'Every flower that blooms has to go through a whole lot of dirt to get there.' Because it's so real to me and reminds me of my own journey and growth, I often use it during my public speaking engagements. Anyway, I had used the quote and was relaxing with a cup of peppermint tea after a gig one day and this man came up to me and said, 'You mentioned that each flower has to go through dirt to blossom, but have you considered that all the nutrients the flower needs for life are in the dirt?' How profound. I mean, I love sayings – by now you know I am the Queen of Sayings. They are how I remember most of the stuff I remember. Words work for me, but those that provoke strong imagery really do it for me. So, this intelligent guy, who thought beyond simply making it through the dirt and out the other side, gives me a whole new slant on things. It is IN the dirt that we get our nourishment. It's actually the dirt and poo that fertilise us and cause us to grow. Without the problems life throws at us, we wouldn't grow, or couldn't grow. The reality is that hard times, represented here as poo, dirt and darkness, CAUSE us to push through and come out blossoming stronger and more vibrant than ever!

My youngest, 'the baby', was telling us recently that she had been reflecting on her life and on how laid-back and easy it had become. She was thinking how simple her days were, without undue threat or challenge. That afternoon she received word that a dear friend of hers had passed away and she was bowled over by the news. It stopped her in her tracks. We sat together and cried and shared some of the details of their friendship, and pondered the difficult walk this poor man had had over many years as he battled cancer. She recalled all the prayers with him and the awkward discussions on such topics as why God allows suffering and pain. She was saying how drained and defeated she felt upon hearing that the disease had finally claimed his life.

At the time of receiving the call, she had been in her lounge room. Stunned, and struggling to process the news, with tears streaming down her face, she had looked outside the window and caught sight of a family of kangaroos (she's the one who lives in the rustic cottage in the bush, and her only neighbours are the wild kangaroos). She thought about her morning routine, which included her and her eldest daughter going out to the lawn and gathering the kangaroo poo so the kids could play without rolling in it, walking it inside, or in the baby's case, eating it. Once a bucket was filled, it was taken around to their garden and used to fertilise the vegetables. She was struck by the realisation that even the poo in life has a purpose. Without fertiliser, her vegetables would be limited in their ability to grow strong and provide nourishment for her family. (By the way, she has a very healthy vegie garden.)

She realised that her contemplation had provided her with some profound insights and challenges about life, and her own spiritual journey. Had she not loved and prayed with this dear friend, and introduced him to God, who knows what further pain he might have been subjected to in the next life. As it was, she was comforted by the reality of God's promises and his faithfulness, trusting that her friend's suffering was well and truly behind him. My daughter felt challenged to remember that her purpose on earth wasn't just to be comfortable and to live for her own enjoyment (of which there was plenty), but to actively share in the struggles and burdens of others, and to encourage them to connect with God and find meaning and purpose for themselves. As she shared this experience and revelation with us, we too felt a similar stirring and challenge to rise.

Without the stuff I used to whinge about, I wouldn't be the person I am today. Without my own hardships and hurdles, I wouldn't have the sympathy or empathy needed to help my 'brothers and sisters' get through theirs. We are here to love. One of the most powerful ways we can return love and show appreciation for this crazy kaleidoscopic gift of life is to continue growing through our dirt and be prepared to reach out and help others through theirs. Who knows, we could all be one giant garden full of colourful, yet uniquely different, flowers.

Sometimes we complicate life when all along it was meant to be so simple. It's not rocket science, that's for sure. We can't give out what we don't have, right? Unless we're committed to personal growth, we haven't got much of worth to give to others, have we? It's a snowball effect. As we grow within ourselves and expand the boundaries of our life, we will find ourselves being able to receive love and give love more freely. The more we give, the more we will receive. The more we receive, the more we will have to give. There's that snowball – and it's getting bigger and bigger! Love really is a beautiful, beautiful thing. Maybe the hippies had it right after all... well, maybe a little bit right.

CHAPTER ELEVEN
seven-second rule

'There is a time for everything – including a time to mourn and a time to laugh.' This must be true because it says so in Ecclesiastes, which was written by King Solomon, the richest and wisest guy in history.

My sister and I have this thing we do. When we're together we head straight for the greeting card section in the supermarket and read all the funny cards. We stand there cracking up laughing, relentlessly shoving cards under the other one's nose, attempting to go one better. We have the time of our lives, and it's absolutely FREE. (Let me add that we always put them back in the right place. I happened to spend a couple of years working part-time as a 'greeting card rep', spending hours tidying up after messy so-and-so's.)

Speaking of cards… I sent a card to my friend Leann a couple of days ago. I had been thinking of her during the night (you know how your mind just goes into overdrive when you really should be sleeping) and I was remembering some of the childishly-silly things we'd done together. After I got out of bed that morning, I jotted down a few of those funny memories on a card, and popped it in the post for her. Just the thought of her receiving it the following day, and the smile it would bring to her face, made me laugh.

Two days later I received a message from her to say she had received my card and was delighted - which cracked me up again. 'Hellooooo Possum, I just got your card in the post, and after a particularly tough morning, it completely brightened my day! Ah the memories. I love the one about me and you taking a week-long road trip and pulling over to take photos of ourselves outside all the places we DIDN'T visit. We cracked ourselves up over that didn't we! And can you imagine the mischief we will get up to in heaven? I reckon God will have a naughty corner set aside for both of us. Kick up those heels sister!' Such an excitable and loveable girl, is our Leann. She is so enthusiastic about well… everything really. Some of us have forgotten the value of letting our hair down, of playing and just being silly for no particular reason. Playing is good for the soul, and there's no rule that says it ever has to end. Many of us need to relearn the art of playing and of having fun just for the pure joy of it. Spend a few hours watching little children and you'll pick up a few tips - after all, they're the experts. By playing and laughing and carrying-on crazy with your friends, you will not only strengthen your relationships, but according to my health guru hubby, you will also enhance your health in every way.

I guess like me, you know some people who are super-serious types, who don't understand the value of laughter, and have even forgotten how to laugh. They're hard to miss - they're the ones who look like they've been sucking lemons for a living. I admit there have been times in my life when laughter seemed the furthest thing from my mind. One solution is to keep a list of all the people, situations, and 'things in general' that are likely to get you loosened-up and laughing. Here's some from my list, but of course, the possibilities are endless: I clown-around with my kids (they can be a ridiculously silly bunch); I get some 'pet therapy' – usually via my grandkids' menagerie, but the local pet shop is always an option; I do something hare-brained or a little risky (I'm proud to say that I'm something of a natural in this regard) like dancing in the rain, or dressing-up like a complete eccentric (op-shops are great for this) and heading out somewhere stuffy and conservative; singing karaoke (have other people pick your songs for you), or skinny-dipping per chance. Sometimes all I need to do is to pick up a 'Far-side' comic, or catch a funny movie, or schedule in time with some of my nutty friends. Whatever pops your cork, as they say.

When I go to the cinema there are two people I like to go with - my sister, or my friend Sylvia. Do you know why? Because both these two laugh easily and loudly, and once they begin, there really is no stopping them. You know the type of person I mean - once they're switched 'on', it's not easy to find the 'off' button. Even if the movie is lame or boring, once these two get started, I find myself getting caught up in the flow - even if it is only them I'm laughing at!

During my days as a journalist we were routinely given WH&S reminders about the need for regular breaks away from the computer and such. The recommendation was to look away from the screen every so often and have a good old stretch; arms, legs, back, shoulders – that sort of stuff. Well I reckon a great big, roaring belly-laugh is just as effective, maybe even better than a stretch. Laugh for seven seconds to start with, and if you feel inclined, keep laughing for as long as you like (or until they come to fit you for a lovely, new, white coat). Your whole body and soul will appreciate your efforts, and, believe it or not, you will be reducing your risk of nasty diseases like cancer and heart-disease in the process. So what are you waiting for?

While laughter is good medicine, shared laughter is even better. My dear hubby isn't a natural laugher, as he is a melancholic type; fairly serious and self-contained if you know what I mean. But throw some of our funny friends in the mix, or a couple of our zany granddaughters, and hubby can become quite the clown. It's good for his soul, and fortunately he's old enough now to recognise when he needs a 'fun-fix', and for the most part, I'm happy to encourage him in it.

A wise man once said, 'Life is too serious to be taken too seriously'. I think that's one of my hubby's quotes - you have to admit it does have a 'ring of truth' about it. Part of me and my hubby's commitment to avoid getting overly serious includes factoring regular R&R times into our schedule - especially times where we can let our hair down, kick up our heels, and have a good laugh at life. One summer night, under a full moon, we climbed out of Buzz, cranked up the music and began to dance. As we grew warmer, we began to peel off our clothes until eventually we were dancing 'au naturale', laughing our heads off at the sight we must have presented. Fortunately, we were far enough away from civilisation not to get ourselves arrested.

I have to tell you about some friends we met in Victoria during our travels. They live on a property with a bushy backyard and enjoy their privacy. It's a very relaxed lifestyle, so relaxed in fact that they often stroll around naked. They told us about an unexpected incident one morning when they were out in their backyard sun-baking totally starkers, just reading and relaxing and lapping-up the warmth of the sun. Without them realising it, a hot-air balloon was fast approaching with half a dozen passengers on board. Turns out, whoever was supposed to be piloting the balloon was so captivated by the sight of this mature couple lying around in their birthday suites that they forgot to watch where they were going. Before they knew it, Renee and Greg had a hot-air balloon stuck in the top of one of the large trees on their property, and the half-dozen people on board were so busy laughing, pointing and gawking at the pair of them running for cover that they could barely keep themselves from falling out of the tree. An entire, lengthy rescue mission ensued. True story.

On another occasion these same friends invited us to dinner. She is a great cook and a wonderful host, and her husband Greg is quite a character. He is your typical Aussie bloke of sixty-odd years of age who loves nothing more than to watch AFL football and drink VB beer. He's a real card, not one to get too emotionally involved in anything, unless of course it involved his footy team - or ABBA as it turns out. Renee had cooked an Italian meal that literally took days to prepare (the depth of flavours she had going on with that meal were astounding, and this was long before our current cooking revolution) and after a nice glass or three of red we retired to the lounge room where Greg had a surprise waiting for us. Turns out this big, six-foot-two, macho, footballin'-man absolutely loved the movie, 'Mamma Mia' and had planned for us all to watch it together. The movie, we were soon to discover, had a cast of well-known actors, and featured some of the best known songs from the ridiculously successful Swedish band ABBA. The movie was a real hit, and as we were getting toward the end, I happened to look over at Greg and he had tears streaming down his face. All of a sudden he jumped up and grabbed me out of my chair and began swinging me around the room, as another old, familiar ABBA song burst forth. We all ended-up dancing together, alternately hugging and laughing and crying, as the final credits rolled on. If you ask Greg about that night I'm not sure whether he would admit to crying over Mamma Mia or deny it ever happened - but we know the truth don't we?

Smiling is definitely the forerunner to laughter, so you may have to start small and simply begin smiling more often (you'll look much more attractive when you smile - unless you've lost all your front teeth). The trick is to retrain yourself and whack a smile on your dial every time you see something or think of something that is even mildly entertaining. As I said, I had to make a list just to kick-start what now comes naturally. At the top of my list, before I could do all those other fun things, was, 'wake up and smile'.

My friend Elaine is a chronic list-maker. Wow, if I'm the quote-queen (and I'm pretty sure I am), then I can assure you she is the absolute queen of lists. I have known her for 18 years and never seen her without one. If there was an award for the 'best and fairest' list maker she would win it hands down. You never see her without a tiny piece of paper (usually purple because purple is her favourite colour), with neat, miniature writing on it, and of course a purple pen in hand to tick each item on completion. I don't think she would be able to get out from between her purple bed-sheets of a morning without her trusty purple list, strategically placed beside her purple alarm clock. Get up (tick), have shower (tick), put on clothes (tick), making sure to include something purple (tick). And you think I'm kidding!

There's an old saying my nana still uses, 'Count your blessings' (I'm sure there's a song about that too – 'Count your blessings, name them one by one, and it will surprise you what the Lord has done...' one of your more 'modern' hymns from the late 1800s). If you struggle with negativity it's a good idea to spend a few moments at the start of each day thinking through all of the things you should be thankful for, jotting them down on paper if need be. It will probably be a much more productive exercise if you don't compare yourself to the rich and famous. Try to be realistic and remember that about a third of the world's population are scratching to feed themselves each day, with no possibility of ever paying-off a house, going on holidays, owning a car, or of having any material possessions other than the clothes on their back.

Once you allow yourself to get past all the things you don't have, and focus your attention on the things you do have, you will quickly see that your list can be quite substantial. As I've already mentioned, being thankful, being positive, and being happy are largely a matter of choice. I used to think that it was all a matter of luck or chance, but the more I look at the lives of successful people, the more I see choice, not circumstance, as the determining factor. If we can get our heads around that truth, imagine what we can make of our lives? Some of us are still waiting for happiness to just show-up, the same way we're waiting for our lotto numbers to be drawn out of the barrel. Don't hold your breath.

Like that Monty Python song from 'The Life of Brian' says, 'Always look on the bright side of life.' We can watch what we say, count our blessings, establish some purpose and meaning for our lives, and we can look outside of ourselves and begin seeing what we have to give, not just get!

One thing I like to do is to ask people, 'What's the funniest thing that's happened to you?' As they retell their story they will start to laugh, and it invariably makes me laugh too. Try it for yourself sometime. Elaine is a really nice lady (even if she is a purple freak), but she has this strange thing happen when she sees someone hurt themselves - she roars with laughter, and you guessed it, almost pees herself. Considering she really hasn't got a mean bone in her body, I think it must be a nervous reaction of sorts. We have seen so many awkward incidents and accidents (like someone tripping on the pavement - usually my hubby) turned into laughter fests that it makes us laugh just thinking about them.

Elaine, Leann and I went op-shopping for some shoes to wear out during one of our holidays together. We all bought ridiculously high heels and then staggered around like drunks because we couldn't keep our balance in them. We were heading out to grab a bite to eat at a restaurant and before we could even get through the front door, Leann had fallen up the stairs. Well, we all lost it. The three of us tumbled into the place wobbling and laughing so hard we almost got thrown out before we even reached our table. Elaine was laughing at Leann falling, I was laughing at Elaine laughing at such an inappropriate time, and Leann was laughing at me laughing at Elaine. Now that I think about it, Leann did look funny tumbling up the steps with her handbag skidding across the floor and her skirt spinning in circles. Fortunately no one was hurt, and that night as we climbed into bed our faces were aching from all the laughing we'd done.

* * *

My hubby and I were camped at Henry Angel Flat when we were awakened by a fox as it gnawed at one of the stay-ropes holding our awning up. We were in Buzz, tucked-up in our cosy bed, when the van started to vibrate slightly and a strange sound came from outside. I looked at my mobile phone to see what time it was. It was just before 5am. Even though it was quite foggy outside, the moon was providing enough light to clearly see this mongrel fox chomping away on our rope. My hubby sat up and proceeded to bang loudly on our side window in an effort to scare it away. The fox didn't move, in fact it didn't even stop to look-up, but continued gnawing at the rope until it began to fray and give way. So hubby jumped out of bed, opened the side door and began to yell, 'Raaar, raaar!' but the fox still didn't move. He looked around for a suitable weapon to give the fox what-for, and grabbing one of our fold-up camp chairs and a stick, started moving towards the fox, waving the chair and stick madly shouting, 'Raaar, raaar!' as loud as he could. He looked a bit like a lion tamer with the chair and the stick in hand. The fox looked up at him, still seemingly unperturbed by my hubby's advances, and its eyes locked onto my hubby's crutch. There was my hubby in all his glory with nothing but a t-shirt on and letting it all hang out, as this cheeky fox eyed his precious manhood. Hubby instinctively drew the chair in as close as he could to protect himself, and after lingering another few seconds, the fox casually trotted off. I don't know whether I was imagining it, but I could have sworn that fox had something of a smirk on its face.

Meantime, the people beside us who were sleeping in the back of their station-wagon, had been woken-up by all the banging and shouting. By the time they looked out into the misty, morning half-light to check out what was going on, all they could see was my husband in nothing but a t-shirt, with his willy dangling, while he roared and waved a stick and chair around in the air. It was quite a sight! The poor buggers next to us must have been frightened out of their wits, as they quickly jumped into the front of their car and high-tailed it out of the camping ground. They made the speediest getaway in history. They must have thought Step was a crazed lunatic. I often wonder what the story sounds like from the other campers' perspective when they tell it to their friends.

CHAPTER TWELVE
view from the road

Current weather report: A maximum of 24 degrees by day, down to minus 12 by night.

It was always our intention to spend the Australian winter months 'up north', as far away from the cold southern winters as we could get. Sometimes life has a way of turning you 180 degrees though (have you noticed that?) and we spent our first three winters on the road, freezing our butts off in temperatures as low as minus 12C. There were more than a few occasions where our nightly attire in Buzz was pretty much everything we owned, including beanies, scarves, gloves, socks and jackets. What we couldn't put on, we'd pile on top of ourselves for extra warmth. At times we had to even cover our faces to be able to breathe the icy air.

One time we were having a whinge about the cold conditions to our middle daughter via a text message, and she reminded us of the saying, 'You can roll the dice, but only God determines how they fall' (from Proverbs 16:33). For some reason (which was only revealed later on) we needed to be right where we were, and not further north where we had hoped to be. So, we pulled up our 'faith socks', and prepared for the best.

And as it turned out, our 40 days and 40 nights spent in Inverell and Tingha were fantastic, and we have many special memories and connections from our time there. We were privileged to be able to 'camp out' in Buzz in the garage of a Christian minister and his family, as it's not uncommon for overnight temperatures to drop to minus fifteen or lower in winter. They insisted we stay inside their spacious home, but we knew that six weeks would have been a big stretch for both us and them, so we made the garage (or the Bat Cave as we preferred to call it) our temporary home.

From the outset we decided to spend four days each week connecting with the town-folk and helping out where we could, and the other days we would explore what the region had to offer in the way of national parks, reserves, lookouts, river-side camps, and 'secret spots' recommended by the locals. We enjoyed the harsh yet unique landscape of the region, with its imposing granite formations, the expansive night skies, the day/night temperature extremes, the exceptional and much-appreciated heat-producing qualities of the local 'box' wood, the unique birds and animals of the region, the plentiful supply of fire wood, and especially the friends-come-family that we made during our brief stay. We spent delightful evenings in welcoming homes enjoying good food and good company as we played cards and shared life experiences.

Sometimes we camp in deep, damp valleys beside chilly mountain streams, and at other times we find some interesting camp sites at the top of mountain ranges. We quickly learnt that these places are not necessarily the best WINTER locations. While the midday conditions are often pleasant and even favorable for walking and doing some exploring, the remainder of the day is usually spent around a roaring fire, hemmed in by thick, blanketing fog. Many mornings we stay in bed, alternately sleeping, making love or reading until the frost and fog clears enough for us to venture out and get the fire going, which in some cases isn't until ten in the morning. At times we brave the conditions, wrap ourselves up in our woolies, and huddle around the fire with a hot cup of chai or a warm ginger delight. As uninviting as it sounds, it is often in places like these that we create some of our more memorable moments.

During our third winter on the road, after spending a challenging yet rewarding couple of months in inland NSW, we decided we would escape the cold for a month or so and journey northward at last. We figured we had earned a good thawing-out, so we set-off for Queensland's Sunshine Coast to catch up with family and friends.

Desperate for an 'ocean fix', we made a bee-line for the coast and ended up staying with family at Lennox Head for a couple of days. As beautiful as Lennox was, after the quiet and solitude of the bush, we found the north coast too busy for our liking, so we decided to take the inland route. After a few hours travel we arrived at Mebbin National Park, where we got to see (and hug) an ancient rain-forest tree, an Arctic Pine, that was said to be 2,000 years old. It was an awe-inspiring experience, and to top it off we took a quick dip in the nearby (invigoratingly cold) mountain stream that fed this impressive giant.

Whether it be wildlife or wild people, we never seem to be alone for very long on the road, which leads me to another one of our bizarre, divine-encounters. When we arrived at Border Ranges National Park (which forms part of The Great Dividing Range, and the border between NSW and Queensland) it was already late in the afternoon and the fog was closing in. We hurriedly gathered some wood (which was quite scarce and frustratingly damp) for a fire. We turned off into what we soon discovered was a car-park for a lookout, and found a secluded place to stay the night. After setting up and getting the fire going we had a quick walk around the immediate area to get a feel for the place. There was a weather shelter in the middle of the area with a big, wooden, picnic table, a fire-place and a stack of neatly-cut, dry wood – a pleasant surprise indeed. We were taken aback to find a swag set up on the table inside the shelter. Somebody had been sleeping here, and by the looks of things, somebody still was. There were no signs of a car or any other form of transport, we were in the middle of nowhere and it was just on dark, so we'd just have to wait until the morning to solve the mystery.

The following morning as we checked the shelter to see if we'd been imagining things, we found that someone was asleep there on the table. Later, while I was collecting wood, I met our mysterious neighbour and he told me he had been dropped up there by his sister, who wasn't due to come back for him until the end of the week – still another four or five days away. Turns out he was trying to come off speed and other drugs and get his life sorted out. He told us he was also a gym junkie with serious eating issues. He felt the only way to get on top of his problems was to be dropped out in the bush for a week with nothing but his swag and some water. It was a deadly-serious, make-or-break time for him. When hunger or cold got the better of him, he would take off walking or running, sometimes for hours at a time, and it didn't matter whether it was midday or 3am. Even though there was plenty of fire wood under the weather shelter, he refused to light a fire to keep himself warm.

By this stage we were really keen to move on as we'd had about all we could take of the cold, but we were concerned about our friend's state of mind, sensing his life was potentially on the line. His sister must have felt the same because on his third day there we got a visit from her, even though it would have been a three or four hour round trip. Her brother happened to be off again on one of his self-punishing expeditions so we talked with her and said we would do what we could to look out for him. We decided then that we would stay on for another couple of days and see what came of it. My hubby made him a beautiful walking stick, and he seemed to be genuinely moved when we gave it to him. Even though he wasn't eating, we invited him over to our campsite each evening after we had finished dinner to join us around the fire, as the cold was pretty intense and had prevented him sleeping each night. We already had had a couple of good raves with him, and as we huddled around a struggling fire he started to share some of the deeper thoughts and issues that had been troubling him.

From our very first encounter we knew we were there for a purpose, and it turned out to be a mission of sorts to help our friend find some meaning and direction in the midst of his struggle. After three nights together we felt it was time to move on. He still had another cold and lonely night before he was scheduled to be picked up, but we were confident that we had done all that we needed to do. We left him with our contact details, some food for thought, and what we like to believe was a loving touch from God. In hindsight, it was obvious that God had wanted to break into his world and we just happened to be in the right place at the right time to deliver the goods. It might not have been our preferred place to be, but we wouldn't have had it any other way. What a privilege.

Within a few days of slowly winding our way further north, we were lying around in our cozzies, soaking up the Queensland sun, all the while busily writing down our thoughts and recording our recent adventures (we both love to write and we believe we're destined to write for a living, which will eventually give us the freedom to travel more extensively). Our month in Queensland was a refreshing time catching up with family members and new and old friends, and of reacquainting ourselves with the salubrious charms of the great Pacific.

And you'd never believe what happened next. We got a call from our eldest daughter offering us permanent part-time work in a new venture their church was kicking off. They made us an offer we couldn't refuse - to run the hospitality side of 'The Olive Tree Art and Coffee House'. And here's the kicker: we would be expected to do the lion's share of the work, with little or no help, for little or no pay! Needless to say we jumped at the offer.

Well, not exactly. Truth be told, we initially turned them down as we weren't sure where we were meant to be, and we didn't want to lock ourselves into something without being absolutely sure it was the right thing.

We had already decided to head south by this time, so we turned inland yet again (God help us, will we ever learn?) and landed in the New England National Park, near Armidale in NSW. It was a beautiful park with some magnificent scenery and picturesque walks – yet surprisingly deserted for a region notorious for bitterly-cold, overnight conditions at the END OF WINTER! Ha-ha. We camped beside a crystal-clear creek - an excellent source of pure, clean drinking water - and firewood was plentiful. Apart from an extended walk in the middle of the day, most of our time was spent collecting wood, sitting by the fire, or marveling at the spectacular night sky. The sky was a mass of pulsating stars that had the appearance of an enormous cascading waterfall reaching all the way down to the ground. The stars seemed so low that, with child-like wonder, you found yourself reaching up to see if you could actually touch one. And as we enjoyed the idyllic setting and the solitude, God started working on our hearts and speaking to us about The Olive Tree venture. After only a few days God had us excited and hooked on the idea.

It was funny really, because during our 40 days in Inverell I had walked past a vacant shop in the CBD of the town on numerous occasions, and for reasons unknown to me at the time, it captured my attention in an unusually forceful way (I had spent more than a bit of time wondering about my fascination for it). I began to see it as an outreach opportunity for the local church there, and I got so pumped about it that I presented the concept to the senior minister. I saw it as an ideal way for the church to connect with the community in a more meaningful and down-to-earth way. I couldn't get the idea of a café out of my mind. The minister told me he didn't think it was for him and his church at that time, yet it continued to pester me. Who would have thought that the 'seed' had been planted within me ready for a phone call from my daughter some months later, from a town some 850 kilometres away. It seems that God planted the idea (and the enthusiasm for it) in me so that when our daughter phoned back asking us to reconsider the offer, it was as if the seed suddenly found 'fertile soil' to grow in…. and grow it did.

The New England National Park lived up to its reputation, and as the overnight temperatures plummeted, we were forced to move on or risk freezing to death. Our second night got down to minus eight degrees and the following night dropped another four degrees. The ice was so thick on our washing-up tub the next morning you could have held an Olympic skating event on it. We vowed that we would be smarter next time and stick to the coast for the winter, or stay as far north as possible. Yeah, we'll see!

And so we headed south again – excited, expectant, and a tad nervous about this surprise, new direction our journey was taking.

CHAPTER THIRTEEN
fantasy of a ten-year-old

Most people we meet on the road during our travels know nothing of our past, nor we of theirs. I am constantly blown away that a lot of the people we meet express delightful 'E' words over our lives – 'you guys are so *enthusiastic, energetic, enjoyable, and encouraging*'. I don't live in denial about my past, or refuse to accept the significance past events had in shaping the woman I am today, but I'm just so busy enjoying this precious gift I've been given that I don't have time to brood about my past. Through grace, I've learnt to accept the journey – take the good with the bad, the great with the sad. And through it all, I recon I can deal with anything now, confident that God will be holding my hand when I need him most.

You might be thinking, 'But Chrissy, you have the dream life - you live in a groovy van, have few responsibilities, and travel at whim.' I mean, I get it... who hasn't yearned for a simple, easy life with freedom from the financial burden of a mortgage and endless bills? Who hasn't dreamt of an uncomplicated life of travel, with days so variable and flexible that it blows the word routine right out of your vocabulary? So I am glad you dared to mention my 'dream life'. Do you know, that before we set out to travel this great nation in our little LiteAce, after selling or giving away everything we owned, I believed we were going to be provided with a spacious, fully-kitted-out mobile home, and an endless supply of money so we would never have another care in the world? After all, we weren't necessarily going to travel for travel's sake, but were going to help people, so why not? We believed we were called to travel as evangelists and to share love with whoever we met, in any way we could (which we still believe). We took our 'mission' from the last verses of Matthew 28 (known as the great commission), where Jesus told his disciples to 'Go'. Go tell people everywhere the 'good news' that God is for them, not against them, and that he loves them. He loves you exactly where you are right now, and just how you are right now. But, part of this good news is that he loves you way too much to leave you where you are right now and how you are right now! He wants to plant dreams and visions in your heart, and he wants you to know the purpose you were made for. He wants you to grow and blossom – just like that garden I've written about.

When a mobile home (or truckloads of money to buy one) wasn't miraculously dropped into our laps, I wasn't a happy camper (excuse the pun). We were setting out, like the Blues Brothers, on our mission from God, but we were in a tiny bed-on-wheels with $400 to our name. Not quite the scenario I had been picturing for years. Most people spend that in a week! It seemed a bit of a joke, and right from the outset I could have easily brooded and got uptight about it. I had good reason to (in my thinking), but I didn't. And here's the key: I accepted my lot in life and I chose to be content, in spite of the disappointment I felt (I spent the first 20 years of my life sulking over disappointments, and I just don't have the time for it anymore).

* * *

I've begun this book in the middle of the story, so now let me tell you about the humble beginnings - the seed (the dream) that was nurtured until it became a reality. From when I was about ten years old I had a make-believe dream where I couldn't wait to go to bed at night so I could fall asleep and lose myself in it. In the dream I would be travelling around Australia (no surprises there) with a school friend of mine, in a double-decker bus. As can only happen in dreams, we would cruise the country and gather stray children. What a funny dream. Mum said I had wanted to be a mum from the moment I could talk. I loved kids, still do. I wanted to help and care for as many as I could. Being only ten, I wouldn't have known how to *make* children, so I simply gathered strays from the highways and byways. In my dream, I had everything I needed in that bus. We taught those kids from school books, and we taught them from our travel experiences. The top deck was filled with beds, and the bottom deck with chairs and desks. It worked so well for me that I kept that dream alive, with various changes, into early adulthood.

It's interesting to note that my passion for travelling Oz and helping people along the way originated so long ago. I had shared it with Step a number of times over the course of our relationship, and after 20 years of me speaking it out, he eventually caught something of it. We agreed that when our kids were old enough and settled enough, we would take off together and see what happened. I remember talking about it until we felt like the idea was something that chose us, rather than us choosing it. It felt so right. We weren't too sure of the details, or logistics, but it excited us both and gave us a common focus beyond the kids. A lot of couples we knew were breaking up once the children left home. They had never really planned anything beyond the children, so once they left there would often be a void that they struggled to fill. During our rocky, tumultuous times, and especially during my breakdown, one of the things that enabled us to draw together and re-kindle our relationship, was that dream. If we want to survive the tough times of life, we must be prepared to use anything and everything to make it through, so don't be afraid to clutch at every straw!

We used to talk and joke about our funny little dream, and as the years went by we would continually fine-tune it. There was nothing too concrete at first, just a rough plan and a sense of excitement to keep us going. Once we believed we were on the right track with it, and realised it was a possibility, we shared it with 'safe' people, people who would support our dream, not squash it. Once we began to speak about our dream more openly the ball began to roll much faster. It's weird how that happens.

If you've had a dream that you've let go of or let drift, I encourage you to resurrect it, breathe life into it, and run it by some visionary people. There's nothing more rewarding than working toward something that makes you feel alive! Don't be afraid of dreaming too big either – if it goes beyond your own lifetime, well, all the better - you may be destined to leave a valuable legacy for the next generation to run with.

A couple of months after sharing our dream with a number of people, I had another dream where I saw myself and hubby beside a van, and there was a slogan written across the side of it. It said, 'Love, Joy & Happy Vibes'. In this dream we were dressed a little bit 'out there', and a little bit feral, if you know what I mean. We seemed to have this supernatural friendliness about us, and we were encouraging people from all walks of life. We were like hippies, spreading the lovin' vibes. We were spreading love, and the joy that comes from knowing God, and people were walking away encouraged, and happy - just like it said on the side of our van. Our eldest daughter actually had that sign *Love, Joy & Happy Vibes* professionally made for us to put it across the side window of our little van before we left. I love that our kids believe in our dreams too, no matter how unconventional they are.

I remember picturing a huge friendship ball, rolling around the nation like a snowball getting bigger and bigger. I get so cut up when I see people struggling through life feeling unworthy, ashamed, lonely or discouraged. I know how much it hurts – I truly have a heart to spread these loving vibes so others can be set free and begin to live to their full potential. The thing about my dreams was that I was really happy in both of them. It was the kind of happiness you feel when you are with all the people you love, at your favourite place, and everyone there is having the best time ever - that kind of deep, inner happiness. I felt so positive that I could almost tangibly feel the incredible potential that was growing within me and 'see' the unlimited possibilities that lay before me. That kind of vision is powerful, motivational stuff!

Anyway, much of this was going down a year or so before we actually set off, and in spite of talking about it and tweaking our plans, nothing out of the ordinary was happening. Have you noticed that? You think it's all going to fit together quickly and easily, but time seems to stand still. We attempted to prepare ourselves in little ways, but it was mostly a waiting game, waiting for the right timing – God's timing. Getting impatient and trying to move things along a bit, we gathered a heap of friends together one day to turn our conservative little van into a hippie-mobile. We provided them with paints and food, and told them to paint whatever they felt like - just make Buzz a happy, colourful van. A young friend of the family, Ryan, was an absolute champion, painting a large Buzz LiteYear across the front.

We bit the bullet and set a departure date. Had we not given ourselves a deadline we might still be sitting around waiting for the perfect mobile home to roll into our driveway, filled with money and supplies for the trip. It was like everything hinged on us having a deadline, and at last things began to move. Maybe nobody else noticed, but we were turned upside down and right-side up. The vision began to get clearer and sayings and quotes popped up everywhere – 'Be ready for action', 'Dreams come true when faith takes flight', 'Great results begin with great expectations', and stuff like that.

We finally set out (spread our wings and began to fly), and yes, it wasn't long before we were broke and desperate for work, ha-ha. Even today we still need to work if we want to keep travelling (some things never change). In spite of everything, we've never lost faith in miraculous provision – we've experienced it far too many times for that - but we are much more pragmatic about how provision comes these days. (Anyway, I reckon there will be a mobile home waiting for me in heaven. You may have a mansion with many rooms, but mine will probably be a home with many wheels.) We've realised you can't be too fussy on the road, especially when your situation gets desperate. If you resolve to do whatever is necessary to get by it usually makes life easier. Learning contentment in every situation is a beneficial life attitude, as Paul said in Philippians 4:12. Some of the jobs we've taken on include fruit-picking, cleaning work (scrubbing motel toilets – yuk), general labouring, fencing, painting, class-room help and café work. Often, we just show up in a town and ask the locals what's available and follow any leads we get. So much for my fantasy life of luxury and ease hey!

The truth is, even though we don't have many of the things the average westerner takes for granted, we still feel very comfortable, even affluent. It may be a different interpretation of affluence, but we always seem to have more than enough. I'm definitely not your stereo-typical female who swoons over clothing and shoe shops and the like (my only 'Achilles heel' as far as shopping goes, is some of the groovy op-shops in places like Melbourne or maybe Newtown). I mean, what do I really need that I haven't already got, and if I do lash out and buy more, where the heck am I going to put it? Living in a car has taught me to be thankful for the basic essentials, and for the most part, it feels like I have more than enough for me. If there's more than enough, then reason would have it that I have enough to share, right? It's my hope you have an attitude of gratitude - I don't think you can ever run out if you are content and have a heart to help others.

* * *

If we understand who we truly are, and if we can align our self-image with that, we will be in the best position to achieve great things, and be in a position to help others do the same. But let's not forget that the 'enemy of our souls' has a big bag of tricks (nothing more than lies and deceptions) to try and keep us right where we are. He wants us to believe that we can't change, can't rise, and can't overcome our crippling limitations. On the contrary, we need to acknowledge our uniqueness and individual giftedness, and be ready, willing and able to contribute our expertise or 'genius', for our own good and the good of all. There is no one who is as well equipped to be you, as you are - you are the 'you' expert! Don't try to be anyone else because it won't work. Imagine if the person you are trying to be is trying to be you. Ha-ha! God knew exactly what he was doing when he created you, and his plan was for you to be fulfilled and happy. He designed us all to live with *enthusiasm, energy, excitement, enjoyment and encouragement - to the extreme!*

My life is such an adventure and my passion is for others to join in the party. I was so far down in the doldrums that the life I have now continues to AMAZE me, so much so that it makes me want to celebrate. And the good thing is I know there's so much more to come. I'm passionate about my life's calling, which is to see YOU rise and be the exceptional individual YOU were created and designed to be - a world changer and a planet shaker. 1800s missionary William Carey, known as the father of modern missions, said, 'Expect great things *from* God, and attempt great things *for* God'. Successful people aren't necessarily more gifted, it's just that they're usually more focused, more passionate and more persistent. So get focused and passionate about something – anything - and stick at it long enough to get the breakthrough you need.

It's a common mistake to think, 'been there, tried that, nothing works'. Man, I got knocked down so many times that I considered hiring myself out for kids' parties as one of those blow-up clowns that are weighted at the bottom – you know the ones that keep rocking back up again every time you punch them in the nose? I felt a lot like that, only I was losing the energy and will-power to get up again (the pop-up clown was deflating). Sometimes life just sucks doesn't it, and you feel like giving up. The 'enemy of our souls' would love nothing more than to see you get knocked down and stay down. You need to keep in mind that you, yes you, my friend, are a winner!

I know that my life (and yours) matters, that we can make a difference for good in the world. A friend once sent me a text with something they had heard, 'I don't think you can make a contribution until you've moved beyond wondering if you're good enough.' So, with this book in hand, and a renewed belief in your value and potential as a person, I have a feeling, a bit of an inkling, that you're in the right place to start living a life of purpose, and because I always pray over what I write, I'm confident that from here on in your life can change for the better.

CHAPTER FOURTEEN
geographical change

I'm not boasting when I tell you I've lost count of the number of people who have encouraged me to write this book. And I'm not exaggerating when I say that I can't recall how many times I've started and then given up part way through when the going gets tough – until now of course! For most of my life I've kept diaries or journals of sorts, so I've already got a massive head-start on a number of potential books up my sleeve. Often, when I've neglected to record the specific details of an incident or happening from long ago, I call upon my hubby to shed some light on the situation. He has an incredible memory for detail and likes to remind me that he is a realist and more reliable a witness than I am when it comes to establishing time-lines and facts. I like to see things as ever-so-slightly-magical. 'No fantasy compares to the magic of my reality', as we have painted across the back of our van.

The new me is a happy-go-lucky, fantasy-bubble girl, who dances through carefree days, where I've got daisies in my hair and laughter on my lips (and after all I've been through, I reckon I have earned the privilege to live this way). Step on the other hand, sees it as his role, his duty even, to pull me up and bring me back to earth. As I've said, we're a match made in heaven - God bless his little cotton socks - and yes, he's also particular about wearing natural fibres against his tender little tootsies and reckons nylon can go straight back to the pit of hell from whence it came.

I often tease my hubby (there's a surprise for you) about the 'Winnie the Pooh' story. I tell him he is like Eeyore the donkey, plodding through life, all concerned with his heavy head hanging down, and I'm Tigger, bouncing around about him all happy and excited. 'Good day, my man,' I exclaim in a loud and cheery sing-song voice on waking. 'What's so good about it' is his reply, as he rolls over and buries his head under his giant pillow. Step doesn't like that comparison. Sure, it's an exaggeration, but he is a dyed-in-the-wool melancholic, and it is sort of close to the truth.

Despite our differences and hang-ups we have somehow managed to support one another, and love and forgive each other, throughout our marriage. He has put up with a good deal from his wild and crazy wife, and has been a rock of stability for his family. He has encouraged me throughout the writing and editing of this book because he knew I had it in me, and he believes in what I have to say - even if he does insist on bringing balance (yawn, yawn) to the equation. In the past, I had set myself goals to write novels, and I had managed to pop out two of them in just as many years, but they weren't that great (actually, in hindsight, I'd say they were pretty crappy, but good practise nevertheless). The problem was they didn't reveal my heart and so they weren't a true reflection of who I am and what I wanted to share. This is.

So in effect, you've got my heart in your hands - my life, my zany memoirs. It's not a chronological record of my life by any means, because that would involve numbers and dates and you already know I'm lousy with that sort of thing (I can barely remember my own age). I actually thought I was 43 for an entire 12 months until I went to celebrate my next birthday (which happens to be April 8th for those who love to send extravagant gifts to their favourite author... I wouldn't knock back a recreational vehicle – nothing over-the-top, just something modest and comfortable. If you need specifics, I'd like one with a bit of a kitchen, and definitely a toilet!). Anyway, it turns out I had only been 42 not 43. I was in a time warp for an entire year, as if the sun stood still and I didn't age at all.

* * *

If 'stock' or 'breeding' is important to you, you will be disappointed with mine – though mum will be disappointed to read that I think my stock's unimpressive - sorry mum. I was raised in a simple fibro dwelling, in a housing-commission area of a working-class suburb of Wollongong NSW. The surrounding districts were full of European migrants, but in my suburb we mostly had 'Ten-pound Poms' from the UK. They were lured out to Australia to help build big projects like our Snowy Mountains Hydro-Electricity Scheme. My dad worked in the steelworks (along with my grandfather, uncles, and later, as they hit working age, both my brothers), and mum was a 'ding-dong' Avon lady (she also delivered meals-on-wheels to the elderly in her spare time). I do have some claim to fame though - I am an *authentic* Aussie, as far as white Anglo-Saxon convicts go. I can trace my criminal ancestry way back to the First Fleet, with the deportation of one Jane Langley to Sydney Australia, for stealing a 'kerchief' (what a terrible punishment – free passage from gloomy old England to sunny Oz).

There was nothing spectacular about my upbringing, and if it wasn't for me being such an extra-ordinary brat it may have been a very ordinary affair. I attended public schools until I had caused so much trouble that I was asked to leave, told to leave actually. Eventually I was whisked away to a private boarding school in the hope that they would make a proper woman of me before it was too late (I'm still divided over whether it worked, or whether my poor folks wasted a terrible lot of money, money they couldn't really afford). During regular school suspensions, with plenty of extra time on my hands, I would hang out with the undesirable boys, the ones who were always up to no good – smoking, fighting, breaking into shops, stealing the school bus when it was full of kids, stuff like that. Between running away from home and spending long periods of time wanting to hurt or kill myself, I recall meetings with DOCS and going on outings with my social worker.

Boarding school was meant to change all that. It didn't help that I almost burnt down the boarding house with a smouldering cigarette butt while secretly having a puff; or that I was caught by the principal smoking in the boys' cricket shed; or that I snuck out of my bedroom window to go midnight motorbike riding with another undesirable - all within my first week. I guess changing locations wasn't necessarily the answer to help me deal with my deep-seated issues, but it was all my poor parents could think to do as nothing else had worked.

Change that will last, genuine change, usually has to come from within. Geographical change rarely does anything other than give us something different to look at. Healing the damaged places in our past usually takes more than a bus trip. We can try to run away but the problem is we take ourselves with us. There was one time in my life though, where the geographical change did help bring about the psychological change I needed. It was about three years into our marriage, maybe four. Up to that point we had been struggling to remove ourselves from the drug scene we were involved in

(Step carried the highly esteemed title of 'Illawarra's Greatest Bonger' and had an undesirable reputation to uphold). We knew there was no future for us as a family if we didn't leave.

We finally bit the bullet and hubby applied for a transfer down the coast, three hours south of where we were living. The company he worked for gave the OK, provided he took a demotion, which meant a pay cut. What a deal, who could resist? It turned out to be one of the best decisions we could have made. We knew nobody and nobody knew us, so we had an opportunity to make a clean break and begin a new lifestyle. Yeah, that was until his first day of work. At the end of the day, a new-found mate offered Step a ride home on the back of his Harley. Upon parking in front of the unit we were renting, he pulled out a bag of dope and asked Step if he'd like a joint or two to welcome him into town. Hubby looked at me longingly and I looked at him with a death-stare. 'No thanks mate, we don't smoke!' was his reply. I know it nearly killed him to choke out those words, but that was the clincher and our new drug-free life began.

* * *

Meanwhile, back at the boarding school in the '70s, God was secretly working on my future, and I was oblivious to his plan. I had formed a most unlikely friendship with a delightfully-toffy, straight-laced, rule-abiding, academic named Karin. I wasn't sure what she saw in me – a rule-breaking, housing-commission-raised, troubled-kid – but I'm glad we connected. Karin is a great friend, faithful to a fault, and generous to boot. Karin has remained a close friend to this day and I'm always grateful for her wisdom, guidance and love. I still shake my head as to what she sees in me, but I now know it was part of a divine plan to provide me with people who would stick by me no matter what. I had no idea how much I would need the stability and unconditional love of a long-time buddy later in life. I have the deepest respect for Karin and her remarkable hubby Wei.

She has been my 'window to the world', having travelled extensively and held leadership positions in many national and international companies. She is one of the most down-to-earth, giving and caring women in my world; a constant source of encouragement, kindness and inspiration. By the way,

Karin and her hubby have written a book together about their experience with 'Doctors Without Borders'. These beautiful people volunteered to live and work in war-torn Angola for a year, caring for the sick and suffering under the most extreme circumstances. You can read about their experience in 'No One Can Stop The Rain' – A chronicle of two foreign aid workers during the Angolan civil war (and of course, all profits go towards funding the ongoing work of Doctors Without Borders). See what I mean about her - she is a saint!

Looking back I can confidently say that Karin was my saving grace at boarding school. For a couple of years she was the sole reason I survived the troubled waters of my life without drowning. In some ways she feels more like a sister to me than a close friend. Back in school though, we must have looked an odd couple. We were chalk and cheese and I bet we had the teachers' tongues wagging and heads shaking during staff-room discussions. Karin had the longest and most neatly-pressed uniform I had ever seen, while I on the other hand sported the shortest uniform the Anglican College had ever seen. Karin did not take on boyfriends as they would have interfered with her studies, while I felt like a beauty queen at a footy match. I was fresh meat for the guys, and they were a rich, new breed I hadn't encountered before – I was in heaven.

Karin's study habits were exemplary, while my study habits were non-existent. Karin topped most classes, diligently followed the advice of her teachers (who loved, respected and adored her), and was compliant with all the rules and requirements of the boarding house. The only reason I can ever remember attending classes at all was to flirt with the 'spunk-rats' (for the uninitiated, that means good-looking guys) who were in those classes. The way some of us link together throughout life here on earth makes me think that God must have a great sense of humour. Karin loved me then, and she loves me still. Had I realised the value of such a rich friendship back then, I may not have contemplated suicide only a couple of years down the track. During that period of my life I was walking around with a heavy, black cloud over my head, unable to see the good things that were happening around about me. I was miserable within myself, and because of that I pretty much hated everyone and everything, preferring to lay the blame for my unhappiness 'out there somewhere'.

CHAPTER FIFTEEN
car accident

At twenty years old I was on a suicide mission.

As you've figured out by now, I wasn't always a happy person, not by a long shot. My self-esteem was low and I walked in self-loathing and self-hatred most of my early days. I disliked myself and feared that most people would do likewise. Because of this fear, I projected bad vibes wherever I went as it gave me a sense of being in control. I would be mean and antagonise others, so that when they hated me, which I believed they inevitably would, I could assure myself it was what I wanted. I would set out to have people reject me, because I lived in fear that people would reject me. Wrap your head around that!

I know now that I'm not Robinson Crusoe as I have met hundreds of people over the last thirty years doing exactly the same thing - in many different ways of course, but always with the same motive and the same sad results. It breaks my heart and it has fuelled my passion to write this book.

Strange as it may sound, I am grateful now for experiencing the pain I did back then. Saying I'm grateful might seem totally weird, but I have been able to draw on my experiences to help so many. I made a deal with myself that the scars of my past would be used as a healing balm for others. In a strange way, I feel like one of the 'lucky ones' to have had a breakdown and been given a second-chance. I could take a fresh look at where I was and where I wanted to be. During the breakdown time, my family loved and supported me by mostly just waiting for me to do what I had to do. To have experienced these healing times with the compassion and understanding of people around me makes me feel very fortunate indeed.

It wasn't quite like that throughout my teens. I was a broken and hurting person. I was full of hurt and resentment. I was angry, mad, furious at life. I felt like I'd been dealt a bad hand and I wanted to punish myself and everyone around me for it.

Have you ever heard of a person called Job? (Not job as in occupation, but Job, the guy in the bible.) Job had some really terrible things happen to him, things you wouldn't wish upon your worst enemy. One of the amazing things about Job's story is that after all the bad things had happened he made the statement, 'what I had always feared could happen, has actually happened' (Job 3:25). Well, I was like that. I would expect life to be shit, and then, surprise, surprise, it was! My self-talk was all negative. The bad vibes I put out had a habit of coming back to me.

I stumbled my way through many boyfriends, demanding so much from them that I eventually drove them away. By the time I hooked-up with a live-in partner, just before my 18th birthday, I was looking to him to complete me. (Tom Cruise would later become famous for using the line, 'You complete me' in the 1996 movie Jerry Maguire, but I'm happy to share it with him.) I was relying heavily on my boyfriend to provide my self-worth. Unfortunately this is a common tale among teenage girls. He was a drug addict when we met, and often dabbled in drug dealing to finance the habit (I knew how to pick 'em!). We lived an 'out of it' existence which was fun at times, but for the most part, depressing. Looking back, I can see why I was drawn to such a lifestyle. Staying wasted allowed me to avoid the harsh reality of people disliking me and rejecting me. I could pretend it didn't matter. I could just get stoned and not have a care in the world. Denial can be a wonderful thing, until it messes you up!

Suffice to say I spent the rest of my teen years living with my boyfriend, drunk and stoned, struggling to pay our bills while we lived the 'high' life. 'Sex, drugs and rock and roll', we had it all. I desperately wanted to be happy, but happiness always seemed to be just out of reach.

Unfortunately underneath the haze of drugs and alcohol was the same girl, with the same unresolved issues - I felt unloved, unworthy, and now, even more unlovely! Nothing had changed ON THE INSIDE. I kept seeking new thrills and new highs, but inside was the same sense of pain, loss and emptiness. It was inevitable that the same old suicidal thoughts would return. When they did, they came upon me with more force and intensity. I was under the illusion that my newfound 'freedom' would make me happy.

For once I was even trying to be genuinely nice to people. I thought I was on the right path and had found the answers to life, yet underneath it all I was miserable. How could I rid myself of this misery? I was paranoid most of the time and I couldn't function under pressure. I was losing it pretty badly at work as I was wasted most of the time and couldn't think straight. I needed to be out of it to handle life, and when I was out of it I couldn't cope with anything. It was a vicious cycle. I was in a bad space. I hadn't renewed any of my old mindsets, so when the going got tough I thought the only way out was to end my life.

I remember being stoned and feeling desperately sad again. I got into my car and drove south from the flat I had been sharing with my partner. The rain was pounding on the windscreen and my tears were flowing freely – how I could see the road is beyond me. I continued driving; contemplating the different options I had for ending my life. After about an hour of driving in the bucketing rain with tears still streaming down my face, I just had to stop. A vacancy sign outside of a motel in the NSW town of Nowra, beckoned me to turn in, so I did. I parked my car and headed for reception. I checked into a room and got myself a little more stoned. I cried some more. I fell to the floor beside the bed in my room, and at eye level I saw a bible on the bedside table, one placed there by the Christian organisation, Gideons International. I looked at that bible and couldn't take my eyes off it. I was fascinated by it and had an overwhelming urge to open it. I had originally set out to take my life, yet there I was, booked into a motel room reading a bible! To this day I still can't recall what I read, but I do know that an audible voice spoke to me while I was alone in that motel room. I'll never forget what I heard. 'Chrissy, this is not the end of your life, this is the beginning!'

The significance and impact of this event completely, totally, changed my life. Nothing would ever be the same from that moment forward. This was the pivotal transformation-point of my life. Wow, God spoke to me, little ol' nothing me, and he was telling me he had a plan for my life.

I slept like a baby that night, and believe me, sleep is not one of my strong points. I rose the next day and drove to my parents' house.

Let me remind you that my lifestyle wasn't the kind that any parent would be proud of. These days not many people bat an eye about a couple living together, but back then, it was frowned upon, especially by my parents' generation. Drugs and alcohol had never been a part of my family upbringing and my sordid lifestyle had to be kept very separate and hidden, if you know what I mean. And, as I've said earlier, mum and I never did have a great bond in the first place. Mum reckons I was born 'a cow of a kid' and went downhill from there. I know for certain that I caused her a lot of grief, as we had lived under the same roof, often alienated from one another.

It's important to mention here that I had experienced a harrowing episode at age 13 that deeply affected me. I had been fishing in a creek near my home with a girlfriend and my younger sister. It was a hot day and we were wearing nothing but our bikinis. One minute we were alone and innocent, and the next a stranger appeared out of nowhere. He began 'helping' us fish, with his hands all over our bodies, until he held a knife to my throat and threatened to kill us if we didn't 'play a little game' with him. Without going into further detail, the ordeal scared the shit out of me and scarred me with a wound I still carry, but what screwed me up even more was the way it was handled. Much later that night, my sister, friend and I had to be interviewed by the police separately. We were bundled into police cars to join in a search for the guy, through club and pub car parks and back to the crime scene and throughout the streets of our once safe little town. As was the practice in those days, mum was told to refrain from mentioning the incident - the fear was that the details would get distorted and our testimonies would not hold weight in court if it ever got to that. We were never allowed to mention the incident again until he was caught and brought to trial – which hasn't happened to this day. It was something that wasn't to be discussed. And so we didn't... and we were left to deal with the trauma of it all – alone.

The isolation and the way things were mishandled definitely made me very suspicious and mistrusting of people for many, many years. I was already vulnerable and a bit screwed up before the incident, but I'm sure that the silence and shame surrounding it added to my relationship woes. Of course, it's easy to see all of this looking back now, but at the time I was just, 'a trouble-maker with lots of hang-ups'. I think the first time mum, my sister and I sat together and brought it out in the open was when I was in my late thirties. I carry a wound within me – it is healed, but not gone. The love of God does heal wounds like that, but a tiny scar remains. I feel fine with the whole scenario now that healing has taken place and we've had the opportunity to talk it through together, and by the grace of God, I truly am at peace with all that happened to me as an innocent girl.

I'm so glad that mum and I are making up for lost time. We're great mates now, and we can probably discuss anything, anywhere, any time. I am proud of my mum and think she is one of the most admirable women in the world. She is not only a brilliant nanna to my kids, but a loving and involved great-nan to my grandchildren. She is very much a part of my life and is always there for family get-togethers. Mum has lived alone for almost ten years since my beautiful daddy passed away, and I find myself hoping that someday mum will end up living with us (I guess that may involve a vehicle a tad larger than our little Buzz, ha-ha). She's a competent, confident woman enjoying an independent life at present, so those thoughts are for down the track somewhere. By then the sales from my books and buckets-full of money from my speaking engagements will probably see me owning a fleet of recreational vehicles; we could simply tow mum behind us in her own little van (the idea of a motorbike and sidecar has crossed my mind should the funds not roll in as fast as we had hoped).

Maybe you've been estranged from someone in your life, someone you would love to reconnect with but you're not sure how. If my story tells you anything it should be that God is in the business of fixing broken lives and broken relationships, and it's NEVER too hard, and it's NEVER too late for him. He's into miracles... they are his domain, his specialty.

Back to the plot... When mum answered the door that day, after my night in the motel in Nowra, I must have looked a mess. I'm not sure where the concept came from but I announced that I was now a Christian and that I wanted to move back in with her and dad. I hadn't prayed any 'sinner's prayer', or 'asked Jesus into my life', but I just knew I'd had an encounter with God and that in my heart I was a different person, with a new purpose. I wasn't the old Chrissy anymore and I knew I had a future. I had no clue as to what that would look like, but I trusted that voice. I had hope for the first time and I hadn't felt so good in my entire life!

Mum nearly died of shock when I announced I was a Christian and was intending to move back home. God bless her. Once I scraped her off the floor she embraced me with loving arms.

I wish I could say I lived happily ever after, but you already know it wasn't that simple. First I had to withdraw from alcohol and drugs, which was traumatic and stressful for both mum and me. Those days and weeks were a blur of confusion and pain, mostly lying in bed with a sore head and weird sensations throughout my entire body. I couldn't hold food down, and I had the shakes. I ended up hospitalised, and it was there, during some of the routine tests, that we discovered I was pregnant. I can assure you that certainly hadn't been a part of my plan.

You see, dear reader, after what I describe to people these days as my 'Saul/Paul conversion' experience, my partner and I were both trying to get over each other with the view to go our separate ways. I had contacted him to tell him about my radical conversion experience and he said that he wasn't interested in all that 'religious stuff'. He was not interested ONE LITTLE BIT. He had been brought up in Catholic schools and reckoned he'd had enough religion to last a lifetime. He didn't want a bar of it. Drug addiction is usually brought on by a variety of things. Some take up addictions almost purposefully, others 'fall' into it. I have a lot to say about addictions, but now is not the time. What I do know, with absolute certainty, is that God CAN and DOES set people free!

The foetus attempting to grow within my malnourished, drug-affected body was our eldest son, the one I was talking about earlier, the one living in the unit at Newcastle, serving in the Australian Airforce. He knows the gory details of his tumultuous beginnings, and is one person who certainly knows he was born for a purpose. He knows beyond a shadow of doubt that he is meant to be here. Accidents do not exist in God's economy; he can turn around what should have been a disaster, and bring forth something beautiful – like our son. When I look back and reflect on that whirlwind time of chaos and confusion, I'm amazed that God chose to use that as the starting point for our new life and our incredible family.

When this oldest son finally reached the age where he could get his driver's license (after many a wide-eyed, white-knuckled lesson from mum teaching him the skills of keeping a car on the road, in the correct lane, at the required speed, without ramming the car in front - 'So sorry Sir'- or puncturing the back left tyre on the curb during reverse parking attempts – 'Yes I do have a spare, son, but no, I don't know how to change it'), he bought himself a cheap yet reliable car from our next-door-neighbour, and headed straight for the big smoke. We were living about three hours' drive from Sydney at the time, and a music festival had lured my son and one of his mates to join thousands of other throbbing teens around the city somewhere.

Later on in the evening, after the music had faded and he was on his way home, he got completely, hopelessly lost. It was inevitable I suppose; a country boy in the big city, in the dark, with no map and no 'Navman' (this was pre-Navman times). He finally found his way out of the city, and after almost four hours of driving he was still an hour from home. Even after stopping for a brief road-side nap south of Wollongong, his mate was quick to fall asleep in the passenger seat, and my son soon followed. With only thirty or forty minutes to home my son's car rocketed off the road, no doubt attempting to determine once and for all whether his car could in fact pass the 'Chitty-Chitty-Bang-Bang' flying test. The car failed dismally, hurtling full speed into a tree then spinning around one-eighty degrees and crashing into another. While every parent's nightmare is the 3am phone call from the police, ours at least was from our son - 'Hi mum, I'm in hospital, I've had an accident.'

My son and his mate, miraculously, were not seriously hurt. The car, on the other hand, was written-off, with every panel of the car, including the roof, badly smashed in. It lay in that paddock for a couple of weeks as a terrible reminder of what could have been, until it was hauled away to the great junkyard at the edge of town. I had snapped a dozen or so photos of my son's smashed-up car for him to view from his recovery bed, as you do, and I distinctly remember him saying, 'I should be dead; I must have survived for a reason.'

When he thinks of the life he lives now, and when he remembers those two particular incidents, he knows he has a purpose for being here on this planet. The truth be told, we all have!

* * *

Between the discovery of pregnancy and the birth of said son all those years ago, my partner proposed that we get married because it was, 'the right thing to do'. His mother had said, 'You've made your bed, now lie in it.' So we whipped-up a wedding on the cheap, which was followed by months of yo-yoing between abstinence and 'using', until our baby son was finally born. There were some complications with the birth, where after twelve hours of labour, he stopped breathing within my womb and was quickly removed by forceps delivery, resuscitated, and placed in a humidicrib for extra care.

It has been quite a journey, a huge journey. How do you describe some of the struggles in life that threaten your sanity and survival? There is so much involved that it is impossible to put into words. The short of it is, my partner became my husband, and my husband eventually became a Christian. Slowly but surely, after years of battling addiction; drug-dealing and drug use were weaned out of our lives. We popped out another four kiddies and went on to foster a few others along the way. We emerged covered with undeserved grace.

Yet, after a miraculous conversion; after discovering real life instead of my wretched excuse for a life; I almost lost myself, another 20 years further down the road, in an emotional breakdown. Sometimes healing comes in an instant – I've seen it. Other times healing comes in waves, over time - when we are ready for it, and when we can cope with it. That's how I've experienced it.

If there was anything I knew by the time of my breakdown, it was that suicidal thoughts and taking myself out just wouldn't cut it. I *had* to recover. I *had* to get up again. I *had* to live the life I was called to live. I knew I had to begin listening and learning a better way, and stop doing it my way. I was a new woman; I didn't need to live like that again. I woke up and began again.

And I may have staggered around at my starting block again, but I had renewed strength. I refused to wimp out. I was determined I would not be defeated. I'd had some setbacks, but I knew beyond a shadow of doubt that I could rise again. I believed I still could be the best *me* I could be. I had more knowledge and experience. I had been brought through some tough experiences and was equipped with plenty of life-skills. I knew what NOT to do, so I figured that was a good starting point to begin to begin again. Without realising it, I had been in training for such a time as this. God hadn't done all that work in me, for all those years, for nothing. I had to wake up, get up and start rebuilding. So that's what I did, but, it was a process, a slow process.

It was during this time that I re-evaluated my life (a breakdown will do that for you – actually, it is *meant* to do that for you), and I realised that some changes had to be made (quick-thinker that I am – 'sharp as a bowling ball', my hubby would say). You may not have had a breakdown and opted out of life as I did, but you may be sick to death of the same-old-same-old of your existence. Some people exist, but never really get to *live*. You may be bored, stuck in a rut, or you may be just 'going through the motions' without any passion or zeal. You may feel like you're going round and around the same old mountain. You may be reading this at a time where you are searching for some answers or solutions on how to get some spice back into your life. Where have all the good times gone? Where has the laughter gone? You may feel like you have been settling for a 'B', when all along an 'A' was planned for you.

I can sometimes recognise this process happening in other people's lives upon meeting them. Somehow we drift from ecstatically happy and switched-on, to mildly enjoying the experience and then, we turn around and, before we know it, life sucks! Just like that.... over a period of time, our oomph, our va va va voom is gone. It's during these times that we need to put the 'super' back into our 'natural', start listening for the right voices, get up and get going and bounce out of our solitary confinement, prepared to take our place in the world. Be encouraged, God delights in every detail of our lives. He has shown me that just being me, as I was designed to be - my talents, abilities and gifts - makes God smile.

I learnt to give up trying to be anyone other than myself. So, taking time to discover who I really am, what I love, what my gifts and talents are, help make me a whole lot better person, and no doubt, more content. I now relax and don't stress over comparing myself to others, I don't try to please them to gain approval. I'm already approved. God loves me just the way I am, but loves me too much to let me stay that way. You see, he's always looking for ways to grow us, to help us become more whole or complete so that we can be all that we were made to be. YOU are God's hand-crafted work-of-art. You are a custom-designed, one-of-a-kind, original MASTERPIECE. Unique. Not one person on the planet is the same.

I reckon our journey begins and ends with love. I don't know if you have noticed, but content people put out great vibes. They love themselves, they are confident with where they're at in life. They are balanced. They don't jeopardise their self-worth by allowing others to use them yet they don't mind helping others. It isn't a weakness to try to understand or empathise with others. Contentment brings love for you and love for others and that's pretty well what life is about anyway. Wouldn't you agree it is worth pondering?

A friend told me about a family that went on a walk by the lake near their home. At one point, the toddler daughter was playing near the lake and slipped into the water. Before anyone had been able to grab her, she drifted further out. The parents didn't know how to swim, so they were in a panic and began yelling and screaming for help. This woman heard all the commotion and the screams and she raced down the bank and into the lake to rescue the little girl. She climbed out on to the bank with the littlie, who, though freaking out, was basically unharmed and OK. Everyone knew it could have been a far different outcome. Yet when the mother grabbed her wet little girl, she turned to the rescuer with irritation, and demanded, 'Where's her hat?'

Let's not be like that. Let's not be so busy looking at the little things that go wrong that we miss the big things going right. So often we listen to temptations or other people's opinions or our own negative self-talk until we convince ourselves we are hard-done-by and can't be happy until things are bigger or better. It causes our focus to remain on small disappointments that keep us grumbling and complaining rather than focusing on the extraordinary things in our lives. It seems extreme that a mother wouldn't rush and grab her daughter and thank the woman who saved her with gratitude and enthusiasm and thankfulness. It seems bizarre she would be ticked off because of a lost hat. Personally, I can barely fathom it. But some people live like that – seeing the worst in everything.

You can't be anyone else; you might as well enjoy being you. Be comfortable and content in your own skin, living with an attitude of gratitude (there's a snappy little saying for you). It doesn't hurt to ask God to show us who we really are, to see ourselves from his perspective. He releases and empowers us to be the best we can be. We can walk with purpose; confidently and powerfully. He provides everything else – gifts, talents, opportunities, connections, provisions – they're all his responsibility.

CHAPTER SIXTEEN
kidnapped

My hubby and I are learning that life is most rewarding when we make ourselves available for others. Having worked and dabbled in various fields for more years than we care to count, and having raised healthy, well-adjusted children, we have a comprehensive range of resources and skills to offer. Without being too precious about ourselves, we simply try to meet the needs of the people we encounter - fill in the gaps, so to speak. Even when we don't have the 'right' skills, we've learnt that it's more about our willingness to lend a hand that encourages people and makes a difference so we simply ask for God's leading to show us where we're meant to be. That might sound super-spiro, but the reality is that we know how much we need guidance and direction, because on our own we'd be lost.

Sometimes though, we get tired and weary and let our guard down. When that happens we can fall for anything that looks good at the time... and yeah, that's when we can get really lost. We were in a little place about 20 or 30kms east of Nimbin in northern NSW a couple of years back, and decided it was getting too late to continue much further. We checked out a dodgy map we had acquired from who knows where (our Navman had recently given up the ghost) and we set off into the hills. We were hoping to stay at the state forest there, but when we arrived it was so wet and muddy and cold that we decided to press on. We drove and drove until it was dark, and then we drove some more. We hadn't had lunch or dinner, and at about 7pm we came to a dead-end up a long, winding, dirt road. We were hopelessly lost!

Needless to say, tempers were frayed so we decided, 'bugger it, we'll stop right here on the side of the road, have a quick sandwich in the dark, and then see if we can find our way out.' We were sitting in the front of Buzz, eating our sandwiches and sipping peppermint tea, when suddenly headlights appeared and caught us in their beam. We were a little nervous about being caught on a private road, but we couldn't put off eating any longer. A car pulled up alongside us and a woman yelled out the window, 'You know you can't camp here!' Already tired and frustrated, we tried to explain our situation - I did all the talking as hubby was too frustrated to speak by now. I explained, as best I could through our car windows, over the noise of her engine, that we were lost. We had accidently stumbled into the predicament we were in.

She got out of her car and came over to help us with directions. We could tell by her accent and manner that she was an Italian woman - a very wound-up, agitated, Italian woman at that. When she looked into the front of Buzz she noticed, amongst many other things, a cross hanging from our rear-view mirror, and asked if we were Christians. We told her we were, and immediately her attitude changed as she assured us that she too was a Christian. Before we could say another word, she insisted that we come back to her place for dinner and to stay the night. Wow, I thought all my Christmases had come at once. I was over the moon and far too enthusiastic to notice Step trying to warn me to be cautious. Without giving him a say in the matter, I was agreeing to follow this stranger up to her property in the hills. I barely noticed that hubby was trying to back out of the deal - my mind was fixed on the thought of a hot meal and an adventure (I might learn to listen to my hubby eventually - one day).

To make a short story long… this woman led us up a wet, slippery, dirt track, unlocking three gates as she went, and promptly locking them again behind us. All the while she was ranting and raving to herself (or to us, we weren't quite sure) about her '*#* neighbours', and how they hated her just because she had dobbed them into the cops for growing weed – 'bloody pot-smoking, no-good hippies'. After the third gate was locked behind us, I could feel the hairs on the back of my neck beginning to stand up, and I glanced at my hubby long enough to see the look of 'I tried to tell you so' in his eyes. When she stopped her car, she motioned for us to pull up behind another two vehicles that were parked at the edge of the driveway. She had told us she lived alone, but there were now three cars other than ours locked up here in the middle of nowhere, where mobile reception was non-existent. Crap, what had I gotten us into now? We did our best to stay calm but we were freaking out inside.

As she waved us up the darkened stairs leading into her house, she warned us to watch out for the big black snake and the smaller brown snakes that were 'everywhere because of all the rats'. What was that about snakes AND rats? We moved warily up the stairs, and even more warily through the front door - and you guessed it, she quickly locked it behind us. Gulp! We were at her mercy! We were locked in her house, with our van locked on her property, and not a sole on the planet knew where we were.

After mentioning again that she lived there alone (where were the owners of all the other cars... in her deep freeze?) she insisted that we have something to eat. There was food everywhere - big pots on the stove, a huge commercial looking fridge and freezer - all seemingly full of food, but no one around to eat any of it. I reminded myself that she was Italian, and as such, would probably love her food. (We had beautiful Italian neighbours some years back and their entire backyard was garden, while their garage, instead of vehicles, housed giant pots of tomatoes and pickled vegies all year round. The largest, thickest, tastiest lasagne I have ever enjoyed came from that Italian family's kitchen).

This Italian woman, much scarier than our ex-neighbours, dragged something out of the enormous freezer and began to heat it up for us to eat. I insisted that it was far too late for me to eat without risking a serious tummy-ache, but Step couldn't refuse for fear of upsetting her. I watched as he slowly and nervously nibbled at what he was given, chewing and swallowing each small mouthful very tentatively. Turns out our host had 'eaten earlier and wasn't hungry at all', which only fed (excuse the pun) our suspicions. It didn't help that each time she picked up one of her large kitchen knives she would think of another story she wanted to share, and like any good Italian, she would let her hands do most of the talking. Focusing intently on her every move, and staying as quiet and still as possible, she had our undivided attention.

The plot thickened as she told us about her life, her family, and some of her escapades in the local community. We were keen to get out of the house and lock ourselves safely in Buzz for the night, but our friend had a captive audience and she wasn't about to let the opportunity slip through her fingers. Man, that lady sure could talk! She told us about her break-and-enter into the Masonic hall two nights prior; about her neighbours wanting to kill her after finding out about her midnight vigilante raids where she would uproot as many marijuana plants as she could from adjoining properties; and of her husband's numerous 'infidelities', paid for on her credit card. She spoke of some of her Italian 'friends' who she could call on to 'take care of business for her' if things got out of hand. Ah, what branch of Christianity exactly did you say you were involved with?

She finally relented and gave in to our pleadings to be allowed to go to bed, and as we cautiously walked back to our van - conscious not to step on any deadly snakes, or trip over one of the hordes of rats that were known to visit from the macadamia farm next door - we tucked ourselves into bed, hubby with makeshift weapons close at hand, and we drifted off into a disturbed and fitful sleep. In the distance we could hear the neighbouring dogs howling at the night, as we imagined snakes and rats crawling up into our van to nest.

At 5am we were awakened with a start as a high-pressure hose hammered onto Buzz. She held that hose on our van, spraying water in all directions, while we scurried around on the bed trying to find our clothes. 'I was just getting all the cow shit off your van - if you leave it too long, the van will rust!' explained this mad woman with her 'weapon' pointed at us. 'Come inside now, I've made a big cooked breakfast for you, and I'm just about to do some fresh juice.' I really had been starving last night, but wasn't game to take her up on her offer for fear of being poisoned. My story sounded fair enough last night, but this morning was different. Step had made it through the night without any dramas hadn't he, so what was I worried about?

She dragged us onto the veranda so we could all sit and watch the sun rise. Even in such a picturesque place, with the prospect of a big breakfast, I struggled to relax. We were handed an enormous glass of juice each – Step reckons they were pint glasses, at the very least. We prayed like crazy over ourselves, trusting in Scriptures like Mark 16:18 'They will be able to handle snakes with safety, and if they drink anything poisonous, it won't hurt them'. We quickly downed the juice while we clutched each other's hand - as though we had some unspoken pact - if we were going to die, we wanted to do it holding hands, and we preferred it to be quick, not drawn out. Scull, scull, scull.

Once our breakfast ordeal was over and done with, we were keen to get away from this crazy, yet surprisingly hospitable, woman. We had listened to her wild tales and put up with her erratic behaviour long enough. The sun was shining, it was a glorious day, and we wanted to get to one of the nearby national parks – and lo and behold, we weren't writhing around in agony with stomach cramps, uncontrollable diarrhoea and vomiting - we were still alive. We hadn't been poisoned, or sliced and diced, and thankfully we hadn't been cruelly dismembered and stuffed into that humungous deep freeze of hers. We hadn't been bitten by deadly vipers, and, despite the threat of being gnawed by filthy vermin as we slept, our faces were still in one piece. We were free, yes free... well, not quite yet. Truth be told, we were released in stages. At first we were instructed to follow her vehicle down the drive and back along the road that we had taken the night before (was that really just last night?). She wouldn't tell us how to get back to civilization, oh no, she wanted to guide us out personally. But first we had to accompany her to a valley 'hidey-hole' she insisted we 'simply must see before parting ways' (did she say parting, or de-parting?).

After parking our vehicles in the bush beside the road, she led us on foot down a wet and slippery, rocky path into a clearing well below the road. We found ourselves standing beside a fast-flowing stream near the bottom of a thunderous waterfall, surrounded on all sides by dense rainforest. Although the scene was beautiful, I was still on edge, with my heart beating wildly in my chest and my ears ringing from the extra adrenaline pumping through me. I kept my eyes on our guide to make sure she wasn't about to produce a weapon or push one of us into the water. Step and I were staying very close together, and I was comforted to see that he had grabbed one of his walking sticks before leaving our van – a useful weapon, just in case.

Hubby and I were clutching hands again, and assuring one another with our eyes that if we ever got out of there alive we would never, ever make ourselves this vulnerable again. Well, I think that's what his eyes were attempting to convey. It was either that or, 'You are going to pay dearly for putting us through this.'

After an hour in the 'bowels of the earth', we convinced our 'kidnapper' to lead us back toward the road. When I saw our vehicle I had to contain an overwhelming urge to make a run for it. Buzz was our ticket to freedom, and we were desperate to get back on the road and away from our kooky friend. Next thing I know Step's in the driver's seat turning the motor over. As Buzz kicked into life a huge sigh of relief involuntarily escaped from my lips. Our abductor, who happened to have a bit of a dickie knee and suspect heart, was struggling up the last incline before reaching the car-park (she wasn't running on the super-powered adrenalin we were firing on). As she made her way towards us, huffing and puffing with the exertion, we knew the window of opportunity for making our getaway was closing fast. And so, with a great display of thanks and appreciation, with big smiles and exuberant waving (and feeling decidedly more grateful for the precious gift of life), we roared away... hoping and praying that we were heading in the right direction. True story!

It's experiences like this one near Nimbin that make me glad we had a solid support network in place before setting out on our 'Mission from God'. We've always had diligent friends and family supporting us through prayer and other means, as we're great believers in the importance of spiritual covering. Many people are sadly unaware of the protection and strength that spiritual covering can provide.

Ray and Wendy are part of said network. Some forty odd years ago, they and their two young boys (and four suitcases) journeyed to Oz from 'The Motherland' as aforementioned 'Ten-pound Poms', which was a reference to the government-subsidised fare from the UK to Australia, by ship. From our first encounter we instantly 'clicked', and even though these guys are around 20 years my senior, they colour my world.

Ray and Wendy are those rare gems in life that become more than friends. Because they have a couple of decades of wisdom on us, they are like surrogate grandparents to our children. They are very close to our hearts, and we consider them more family than friends. They pray for us every day, yes, every day. That's some crazy commitment there! They sow into our dream and they smother us with love and support in every way they can. We learn so much from this couple and we adore them. They are interesting and funny (that's funny ha-ha and funny strange), and although they are quite opposite in so many ways, they both share a love for helping others. Wendy and Step spend hours talking health matters while Ray and I talk about... hmmm I'm not sure what we talk about. Time flies when we are together – Ray, like me, loves attention, so basically, we don't care what we talk about, so long as we're together talking ha-ha.

Along with our Pommie friends Ray and Wendy, our friend Chris is another essential member of our support network. Not only is she a super prayer warrior, but she's also a real groover on the dance floor – a good balance wouldn't you agree - and once she gets going, she loves a good laugh almost as much as I do. Chris is one of those 'behind-the-scenes' people who play a vital role in church life, providing much of that covering and support I mentioned. Being a prayer warrior and a long-time intercessor (that's someone who stands in the gap and prays on behalf of others) Chris is someone we call on when things get tough. Often we'll just send her a text message to let her know the town or situation we are in and ask her to pray and help us find the best way forward. She sends us scriptures and often leads us very specifically in how we need to deal with the circumstances we're facing. She is a faithful friend who has helped us through numerous sticky situations including debilitating sickness in Bourke, trying to dodge a nasty stalker in Queensland, or helping us solve a major family crisis in Victoria. We have been mates for a long time and we trust her judgements, knowing that God speaks to her, and through her. Her wisdom and sound advice have seen us through some really heavy stuff. She is a rare sparkling jewel. If I was into labelling buddies (and obviously I am) she would be my 'faith' friend. Faith is the key that unlocks the storehouse to all God's splendid resources.

What a journey we are on. Many doors have been opened to us - some that we hadn't even thought about knocking on. Almost everywhere we go we meet random strangers who we add to our friends (no, our 'nice-but-decidedly-crazy-lady' near Nimbin did not get our forwarding address). I totally love my life. I'm enthusiastic about it. I don't want to miss anything.

While we haven't got money to fall back on in a crisis, our faith that we're in good hands has pulled us through more times than I can remember. When we trip over ourselves (which is more often than we'd like), God is always there to help us get back on our feet again. It's fun. It's unconventional. It's crazy (and yes, often a little scary too)! The truth is, living life on the edge the way we often do, can make you a nervous wreck if you're not careful, but taking a step backward after taking a step forward doesn't have to be a disaster, it's more like a cha-cha.

It's easy to think that a 'rich person' is the one who has the most… but the reality is, a genuinely rich person is the one who needs the least. If that's the case, I'm absolutely loaded! We've learnt the wisdom in GK Chesterton's words, 'There are two ways to get enough. One is to continue to accumulate more and more. The other is to desire less.'

Sure, we struggle at times, but we get to experience loads of luxuries. The places we go, the people we meet, and the adventures we have, have filled more than a dozen journals - and we're only part-way through the journey. We pinch ourselves sometimes. We can't believe this is our life... and we have never been without the basic necessities of life. We always have a warm bed to snuggle in; our camp-fire food is generally nothing short of gourmet; and we're fortunate in that we love the 'groovy threads' we can pick up from op-shops along the way. We are hopeful that the funds we raise from this book (and others) will catapult us into the next leg of the journey - so, a big thank you for playing a part in our vision as I encourage you in yours. Odds are you're not silly enough to take off in a pokey little van without any money; but whatever it is you wish you could do, I pray this book inspires and motivates you to do it. As a matter of fact, I DARE you to do it! But before you rush off into the fray, make sure you finish this book first, as it'll give you the 'heads-up' and hopefully make it easier to pursue your dreams. And whatever you do, remember the value in having a network of people behind you who will support and encourage you in achieving those dreams.

CHAPTER SEVENTEEN
time out

It is 3am on a Thursday and I'm typing this in semi-darkness while the rest of the world slumbers. There's barely a sound, it's so peaceful. I've never been a great sleeper, so this is my standard switched-on, active brain time. I rarely do 'all-nighters' of sleep, so writing in the early hours while the world dozes on oblivious, is probably more the 'norm' than a sacrifice. This is MY time. I love tapping away at the keys of my laptop, or where power isn't available, I'm equally happy writing longhand. Both of these options are a welcome relief from tossing and turning in bed, waiting for dawn to arrive. Once I've prayed for everyone in my known universe, I run out of things to think about, so I get up (or simply roll over and switch on my battery-powered headlamp) and write.

During this phase in my journey, it's the middle of my working week and I have to be up bright and early for work tomorrow, so I don't want to linger too long writing, as sleep, though spasmodic and erratic, remains an essential of life, even for this little black duck. I can't afford to carry on like a bear with a sore head where I work, as we're all about trying to make people feel special. I call it 'work' more for your benefit than mine, as I don't consider it work – it's really part of my life's calling.

At the time of writing this, my hubby and I are 'planted' in Batemans Bay serving in the coffee house I mentioned. I spend my days serving and enjoying the company of customers-come-friends, and love it with a passion. My hubby makes most of the food and cuppas, and in-between tasks when he has a spare moment, joins the frivolity outside of the kitchen. The Olive Tree Art and Coffee House (affectionately known as The Tree), is an initiative of the church that our daughter and son-in-love lead (I know he secretly loves it when I refer to him as my 'son-in-love', but ask him and he will deny it – every time!). The church pays the bills, while we do our bit and serve. It is our 'thing' at this present time. We are working within our gifting and fulfilling our purpose, and for the most part, we feel it's a privilege to be serving our community - offering love, friendship and a listening ear, and importantly, a damn good feed and cup of coffee (though my preferred brew is organic chai tea, brewed in whipped organic soy milk, sweetened with local honey - yum). The Tree is unique in that it offers 'food' for the whole person.

The gallery is situated within close proximity to the CBD of the town, and as Step and I seem to click with most people there's always plenty of people to love on and connect with. We serve side-by-side (which suits us perfectly – most of the time), as we try to represent what God (and our church) is all about - and that is connecting people with people, and supporting and encouraging one another to be all that we can be - body, soul and spirit.

That brings me to the question many people are compelled to ask, 'How on earth do you not kill one another when you live and work together in such close quarters?' Because we are literally side-by-side so much, the truth is we do drive each other crazy at times, and yes, the thought of killing my hubby has crossed my mind, and, from the words and looks we occasionally exchange, I'm pretty sure my hubby has had similar leanings. But really, isn't that normal for any good, long-term marriage anyway?

One thing we have learnt to do though (to minimise the risk of bloodshed and/or a lengthy custodial sentence), is to give each other more personal space. Step goes off surfing or exploring, whittles walking sticks, plays his ukulele (I don't mind missing *that*), or just hangs out with a mate doing blokey things. I on the other hand, simply need time out with the girls, either at the movies or over lunch. Even when we aren't able to get the physical distance between us that we need, we have an understanding that allows us to withdraw into our own space, doing our own thing without interruptions or demands from the other. One of our best forms of escape is to lose ourselves in writing or reading, which we both love, and invariably do on a regular basis. When it's all said and done, we probably get on better now than we ever have, and while we still bust out and have a 'barney' in front of family or friends on the odd occasion, we generally enjoy each other's company and miss each other when we're apart.

We did 'normal' life for a long time. We were there together (all bar one 'hiccup' period when I lost the plot) throughout the years our five kids were growing up and needed us. We worked and played and studied (Step did the studying and I did the playing), and life flowed on. After years of sharing the countless life-shaping experiences that make each family unique, which for us included a few foster kids thrown into the mix here and there, our kids began to stand on their own two feet, and one by one, they headed out to find their place in the world.

As you can well imagine, things are very different now since we took off on this crazy adventure five years back. We are stuck like glue to one another, 'joined at the hip' almost 24/7, alternately driving each other crazy, and being the best of buddies. It's a funny set-up which works beautifully - most of the time. We volunteer three days each week at The Tree, and the other days we can drive away in our little house-on-wheels and sleep on a beach or in the bush. It doesn't always work that simply of course, as we still have to earn a few extra bucks to keep the wolf from the door, so some of those 'days off' can be spent working.

When we do get away on our escapades, one of the best things about it is that we don't have to keep regular hours or be locked into a routine. Mostly we just write, read, play, eat and sleep. We tumble into or out of bed any time we feel like it; we walk, swim or jog; play cards; read or write; go surfing or fishing; or we might just sit around mesmerised by the fire. It's not unusual for us to chill-out together for hour after blissful hour without saying a word, just drinking-in the soul-soothing sights and sounds of nature. We have camped near streams, rivers, dams and oceans; in dry Eucalypt bush and thick, damp rainforest; in National Parks and rest areas; within eerie, misty valleys and on 180degree-view mountaintops. Sometimes, in the remote places we meander into and stay a while, the only life we see is the Aussie-bush kind; koalas, kangaroos, emus, foxes, possums, bandicoots and birds. We realise just how healing these times are, and so we try to make them a regular inclusion in the diary. Maybe you're reading this and a few lights are going on. If you know you need to prioritise some time-out, just do it, what are you waiting for?

Even though our original plan included travelling Australia whilst sharing loving vibes, we didn't want to be in too big a hurry, but preferred the idea of taking our time to really experience the country, not just see it 'on the fly'. You hear of people who jump in their car with a lovely modern van in tow, and zoom around the country in a month or two without ever seeing anything outside of a comfortable van park. Their goal is to 'do the lap' without much thought about seeing the real Oz. To each their own, but that's never appealed to us. We travel at a snail's pace. We've been 'travelling' for years and have barely seen NSW and Victoria, and only titbits of Queensland and Western Australia. We haven't even started on Northern Territory, South Australia or Tasmania. Admittedly, we do tend to stay in certain places for weeks or months (or years) at a time, which makes all the difference. And, we're forever being drawn back to the South Coast where so many of our kids and grandkids are. It's a delightful predicament to be in.

We may not get far, but we are *in* and *on* the journey. This, right here and right now, is part of it. We might have a lot of Australia left to see - almost all of it - yet we have 'seen' so much already. It's all about perspective, isn't it? We kick around in places long enough so that we can actually experience that town or that part of the country. And because of that difference, in some of those towns, we can make a difference. We don't just visit them; we attempt to be agents of change in our own small way. We believe that the help we offer, even though relatively insignificant, allows the grace of God to visit and impact that place in a lasting way – whether we see any difference with our natural eyes or not. We may not be world-changers, but we do help to change some people's world. If we didn't believe it, we wouldn't do it.

Recently, one of our Olive Tree customers, who over the last six months has become like family to us, joined us in church. I ended up holding her hand and introducing her to God - as simple and as beautiful as that. When I'm a part of something like that, it makes me want to celebrate. For me, there's nothing that compares to helping people connect with God. More than a few times Jesus talked about the celebrations that happen in heaven as people come back to God. I'm convinced that heaven is nothing like many people imagine it to be. I think the title of one of Tony Campolo's books, 'The Kingdom of God is a Party', gives us a more accurate view of heaven. If you don't believe me, have a look at Luke 15. I'll write more on this, but for now suffice to say that the story about the prodigal son and his return home gives us some idea of the longing within the heart of God to have us all close by him. He wants us close so that he can love on us, provide for us, and know that we are safe. That's why there is a party in heaven over every lost soul who comes back to the father. Yahoo, what a delight to be linked to another party breaking out in heaven!

Like I said earlier, we're like the Blues Brothers on our Mission from God (minus the wild car chase, nuns chastising us with rulers, and a few expletives). Whatever shape and form our mission takes is fine by us. We learnt fairly quickly not to try and conjure things up, but to let them unfold as we go along. We always get shown what to do and we have experienced some memorable moments. We have been invited onto Aboriginal missions, volunteered in crisis centres, lent support in various communities and churches, helped raise funds for worthwhile projects, served as classroom aides in an Indigenous school, volunteered on teams serving refugee camps, distributed shoes and clothing to the needy, just to name a few.

Like anyone else though, we've been through our fair share of good times and bad times; times where everything seems rosy, and times where life sucks hard. We've had times of plenty, where friends (new and old) have welcomed us into their fold and treated us like royalty – putting us up in five-star luxury accommodation, and spoiling us like kings and queens. At other times, we've felt alone and isolated, poor and desperate, over-worked and under-valued, and more. Truth be told, we have thought about quitting. But because we believe in what we're doing, we're determined to see it through – or die trying, as they say. A word of warning; unless you are fully committed to what you are doing, it's easy to allow circumstances or feelings to get in the way and derail your plans.

Perseverance means hanging in there, refusing to give up. Understand that purpose and destiny are far bigger than circumstances. It's usually not our circumstances that hold us back, it's what we do, or don't do, about our circumstances. It isn't what happens to us, but how we react to what happens to us. Every now and then it's wise to stop and take stock of things - have a look at yourself and assess whether you're under too much pressure and stress, and if you are, grab some R&R. Well-timed rest or play can allow you to catch your breath, and before you know it, the clouds part and you see that the sun was shining all along. You have dreams to fulfil and a purpose to live for, and your chances of succeeding are, to a large degree dependent on developing good personal-management skills. You get to choose whether you stay and fight for what's yours, or whether you quit and settle for the mediocre existence of so many others.

In and through it all, we're learning some great life principles, and drawing away to a quiet place where we can recharge and refocus is just one of them. If you look at the gospel accounts of Jesus' life in the New Testament (Matthew, Mark, Luke and John), you'll see that he understood the importance of 'time-out' more than most. I don't know about you, but I find it's so easy to get side-tracked and a little 'lost' if I stay in the thick of it for too long without a break. So whether you're seeking wisdom for the next leg of the journey, or trying to get fresh perspective on something, or simply allowing yourself time to regenerate, time-out is an essential commodity that you can ill-afford to be without. And while you're at it, why not treat yourself to a bloody good laugh.

CHAPTER EIGHTEEN
get the giggles

One day not long back on our travels, hubby and I passed the funniest little car we've seen for a long time. It was like the blue Reliant Regal three-wheeler car you see in Mr Bean skits, the one he was always doing battle with. It just didn't look real. And it certainly didn't look like something you would be allowed to register or drive on the road. It was cute and zany and comical, like a cartoon replica of a vehicle. It so tickled our fancy that we started laughing. And before we knew it, we couldn't stop. We got the giggles over it. We would laugh and laugh, with tears streaming down our faces until we were exhausted and forced to stop to get some air back into our lungs. Then one of us would look at the other and we would start again. It was hilarious. We couldn't control the laughter. We had been on our way to a restaurant for dinner and we knew we needed to act a little bit civilised, but this just added to the humour of the whole situation. Tumbling out of a technicolour van laughing our heads off could look a little too much like foul play - the 1978 Cheech and Chong 'Up in Smoke' kind of foul play - if you know what I mean. What with hubby's dreadlocks and all, onlookers could have been excused for presuming some illicit substances had been on the pre-dinner menu.

We sat in that posh restaurant that night attempting to eat our sizzling garlic prawn entrees and chicken cordon bleu mains between bouts of spontaneous laughter. I have no idea what the other diners thought as we were beyond caring, but I can assure you it was one of our more cleansing, exhilarating, and decidedly relaxing evenings.

How about you, do you need another laughter break? If you're getting weary and bogged down; if you're starting to take life, and yourself, too seriously, here's what you can do. Start laughing. I mean now. Yes, right now. Laugh. Keep going for seven seconds. If you're reading this on public transport it's even better. I can pretty well guarantee that after seven seconds of laughter, you will either have scared the crap out of the poor buggers sitting around you, or have them laughing along with you. Laughter is infectious. The sound of laughter is far more contagious than any cough, sneeze or sniffle. I reckon if there's an infectious epidemic doing the rounds; laughter is definitely the one to catch. When you share laughter with someone else, it brings you together, and rather than being reduced through the sharing, it's somehow magically increased. A good sense of humour is still one of the most powerful tools we have for supporting healthy moods and emotional states (see, I still remember fragments of what I half-learnt during my half-completed counselling course).

So right now, as you laugh, know that this laughter is triggering healthy physiological changes in your body. Keep in mind that your mind is the 'driver' of your body, so anything that benefits or improves your head-space, will always bring about positive, flow-on benefits for your physical body. How cool is that. There is so much of life that we can control if we choose to - we just need to be more aware and switched-on to our potential. Laughter has been proven to strengthen your immune system, boost your energy levels, reduce pain, and protect you from the damaging effects of stress. Laughter is free and laughter is fun. It's available anywhere and anytime, and it's a medicine you don't need a prescription for. I've heard it said, from a fairly reliable source, that a good laugh (let's say the seven-second one I keep harping on about) can cause the muscles throughout your entire body to noticeably relax for up to 45 minutes afterwards - for real!

I like to begin my day with laughter. Maybe seven really is a magical number, because after seven seconds something seems to break, and before I know it I really feel like laughing more and more. I sent hubby a text from the beach yesterday, 'It's going to be a good day, nay a great day... I'm already filled with wonder, sunshine and laughter. I'm meandering along the beach, staggering like a drunkard, laughing out loud like a jolly lunatic. I tried to stop at seven seconds but it keeps bubbling up from within me and expressing itself in great guffaws.' And when the two of us met up later, we had another chuckle about the absurdity and silliness of it all. Laughter is wonderful. That's why I love my friends Dale, Susan, Leann and Elaine – people who understand the value of a good belly-laugh.

If Karin is my sophisticated, worldly friend (that's 'worldly' in the best and nicest sense of the word) from boarding-school days, where I flopped around like a fish out of water, then Dale is my 'smart' friend. We've been buddies since our early teens, and when I say *smart*, I really mean she is a freaking genius. Of course that doesn't mean Dale and I always made *smart* choices back in our teens, does it? We were your typical ratbag kids with our fair share of rebelliousness and naughtiness, and there were more than a few mums who warned their daughters (and sons) about us. Not surprisingly though, Dale is a pillar of society now, holding down a senior administrative position in health, where among other things, she writes responses to MPs and Parliamentary Questions, some of which are curly media issues, on behalf of the Minister and her team. I on the other hand, still have mums warning their daughters to stay away from me. Ha-ha, kidding!

Our friendship has spanned many years and remains a great source of richness and joy to this day. You know those people who you can instantly be yourself with. There's no need for airs and graces, or pretences, it's just straight into where you left off the last conversation, whether it was two days or two years ago. I was with her a couple of months back and our 'big mission' was to get a photo of ourselves together so that we could post it on Facebook. You see, we think that everyone else we went to school with has aged dramatically, but as for us - we are still hot chicks! Do you think we could click a photo of ourselves that we both approved of? We were laughing so hard by the end of it our hubbies thought we'd gone mad. And we *are* mad when we're together. It's the fun of being long-term mates. Dale is beautiful - she still gets her nails and hair done regularly, exercises at the gym, and wears smart and sexy clothing. She is one of the funnest people I know - who else would take a dip in the ocean at 1am with a couple of male friends, or make a bit of a spectacle of herself at her daughter's 21st birthday party by deciding she should do the splits in the middle of the dance floor – but as Dale says in her own defence, 'it was very late'.

Good friendships are important as they help us through many of life's struggles, and in turn, they give us an opportunity to respond with love, understanding and loyalty when it's needed. A couple of these close-to-my-heart, long-standing friends are Leann and Elaine; as mentioned throughout this book. Leann is musical (sings like a bird), funny, eccentric, outrageous, creative and artistic, and great value all round. She is what I lovingly refer to as my 'short' friend. She is so tiny you could pick her up and pop her in your pocket. But what she lacks in height, she certainly makes up for in noise!

When we get together we are loudly-rowdy, or rowdy-loud (I'm not sure which – maybe both), and we are inclined to show-off whenever we get the slightest opportunity. When we're in the room, everybody has to know it. Not to do things by halves, we actually like to imagine that everyone in the room is there *for us* (I know this is a kind of crazy, narcissistic delusion we are under, but it works for us). When the opportunity arises, we travel about like Thelma and Louise, having wild and crazy adventures together, and it's not just because we love being together, it's because we need more stories to share with our 'adoring fans'. (My hubby suggests intensive, long-term therapy, but I say, 'Baby, ease-up on your melancholic attitude and sit back and enjoy the fun us sanguine extroverts can provide for you.')

One time, Leann and I caught a plane from Sydney, NSW, to the Sunshine Coast, Queensland. We introduced ourselves to the air-stewards, and of course, by the end of the trip, they were introducing us to the pilot. On that particular trip we had been working on a portfolio of 'toilet photos' (we like to have themes for our holidays, and this one was 'photos of toilets' – surely you've done that?). After explaining our theme to one of the air-stewards, Roger, he was thrilled to be invited in on the caper (Poor Roger, I think he thought we were famous and were giving him his fifteen-minute-claim-to-fame opportunity). Next thing we knew, the three of us were crammed into the plane's tiny toilet compartment while one of the other stewards was clicking away on Leann's camera. Roger, obviously a real lover of adventure (and not far away from the unemployment queue), came up with other photo ideas, such as us with multiple oxygen masks on and life-jackets strapped around us. It was a fun time as we laughed, sung, showed-off, and generally provided the on-board entertainment for the hour and a half flight. We had the 'audience' captivated (probably more captive than captivated, if the truth be told), and at the end of the journey the entire plane-load of people applauded us. True story! And my dear 'wet blanket' of a hubby had the audacity to suggest that they were probably clapping so enthusiastically because they knew their ordeal was finally over. Who knows, could be a new take on one of those disaster movies – 'Airport 17'.

Elaine is another of my good friends, and she has earned the coveted label of my 'gossip' friend (that's gossip in a GOOD way, not to be confused with the 'Dorrie Evans' style of gossiping). She never talks down or bad about anyone, but she always knows EVERYTHING that's going on. I don't know how she does it. She seems to have a built-in radar for news - who just married whom; who just had their third baby, by C-section; who got the promotion to 2IC of the RAS; and did you know that Lisa just won $1,524 in the State lottery?... there's not much she misses, that's for sure.

To be fair, I suppose she is more a detail-queen than a gossip. Whatever you do, don't ask her a simple question like, 'What did you do after you finished work today?' because the story will begin from when she woke up that morning, and will include essential details like what she had for breakfast, what she wore, whether it needed to be ironed or not, what she was listening to while driving into work, the office dramas she had to cope with that day, and if you're lucky, she may even eventually get to what she did after work. You know the phrase, 'to cut a long story short', well Elaine has a gift for doing just the opposite. Though she can talk the leg off a chair, amazingly, she is also a pretty good listener. I guess that's how she knows so much about people. But more than anything else, she is an even better laugher. I've been friends with Elaine for 18 years now, and at least once a year (and I'm being very kind here), she laughs so hard that she starts to cough and choke and has tears streaming down her contorted face (picture Linda Blair from 'The Exorcist' and you're getting warm), and then she pees her pants. Elaine is good value and as you can gather, all class! I couldn't survive without her. She often spends Christmas with us, and is happy to take videos and photos of the day. She loves people. She loves me. She loves my family. I think she is the bee's knees and the ant's pants, and I look forward to every visit, and every long, lengthy, detailed, drawn-out (help me) phone call.

Step has always been a friendly person, and people are naturally drawn to him. Fortunately, hubby and I attract friends wherever we go now. Susan is one such friend that I've made along the way. She's my 'proper lady' friend. She's always immaculately dressed, with all the right accessories: feather boas, chunky jewellery, and dangly, sparkling earrings; and I don't think I've ever seen her without a perfect make-up job. She rarely has a hair out of place, looks stunningly gorgeous (somewhat like Liza Minnelli in her prime), and she's one of those people who appreciate their appearance without being a poser about it. She's hot stuff and well aware of her feminine charms, but never uses them to get her way, except with her adoring hubby who is mere putty in her hands. She is beautiful on the outside, but her true beauty shines from the inside. She has a caring heart, and ultimately, it's the way she loves, not just looks, that is so attractive about her.

Whenever she's indoors, Susan gets around in her wheelchair, otherwise she's hooning about on her souped-up, canary-yellow, motorised scooter - the unfortunate result of contracting polio as a child. Sure, there are a few challenges as a result, but she and her hubby take it all in their stride without complaining – whereas I on the other hand, would be whingeing like a stuck pig. Susan is refined and cultured, yet she has no problems letting her hair down and having fun. For someone who is wheelchair-bound, she sure makes some mighty fine moves on the dance floor – kicking up her 'wheels' if you like. Just one tip though – make sure you stand well back when she pulls off those 360's on her back wheels – it can be deadly if you're dancing too close. Susan has a sharp and enquiring mind and likes to keep me up-to-date with what's happening in the world, even though she knows I'll probably forget it all by the morrow. Graciously, she never points out what an airhead I can be, but allows me to feel more knowledgeable and 'with-it' than I deserve. For two chicks that only met five years back, we have a super friendship and it feels like we've known each other all our lives.

Friendship is a gift. I know I can't make it through without the love and support I receive from others, and I hope you're realising the same for yourself. We need friends if we want to be a healthy, whole individual, we can't do it alone, that's for sure. And the great thing about these dear friends of mine is that there is hardly ever a get-together without loads of laughter.

* * *

The Encyclopaedia Britannica, those weighty volumes which used to take pride of place in everyone's lounge-room bookcase when I was growing up, describe laughter as, 'rhythmic, vocalised, expiratory and involuntary actions'. Technically, fifteen facial muscles contract, including the zygomatic muscles. Meanwhile the respiratory system is affected as the epiglottis half-closes the larynx, so that air intake occurs irregularly, making you gasp. In extreme circumstances (like Elaine) the tear ducts are activated, and while the mouth is opening and closing and the struggle for oxygen intake continues, the face tends to become moist and red. There may also be reduced pelvic-floor control, with a loosening of the bladder sphincter muscle in particular – which typically results in, you guessed it, peeing of the pants (and yes, that's

Elaine again). The noises which can accompany this bizarre behaviour range from sedate giggles, to boisterous guffaws. But who wants to get technical? Let's just laugh and enjoy the experience.

Did you know that the happiest and most contented people in the world are usually those that are the most giving and the most grateful? Isn't that interesting? My son-in-love, the minister (the one, 'with his own parish', according to my mother-in-law), tells me that, if we did nothing else in life but worship God and serve others, we would be living out our life's purpose. Another friend of mine put this theory to the test for herself.

Right from an early age, Mel had been diagnosed with depression. One of the biggest things she struggled with was feeling excluded or 'left out'. She felt she was the least loved child by her parents, and the most unloved and least-connected of her siblings. She had been taking anti-depressants for many years, and as a consequence, usually felt 'flat' and listless, and tended to struggle with her weight. One of her regular complaints was that nobody came to see her, and virtually nobody bothered to phone her. If you met her today though, you would be hard-pressed to see those old traits in her. She has become much more positive these days, and understands the value of getting actively involved in her community. She walks daily, is losing weight, and is one of the most generous people I know. She now helps coordinate Operation Christmas Child in her town, through an international relief organisation called Samaritans Purse. Each October, 'shoeboxes' are generously filled with toys, books, pencils and personal hygiene items, and then sent to children in under-privileged countries, just in time for Christmas (a powerful message of love and compassion that never fails to bless the givers as much as it blesses those darling children on the receiving end).

The turning point for Mel came soon after she had spent an enforced stint in the 'psych' ward of a mental-health facility. She was determined to turn her situation around and to take the necessary steps to ensure her future was different from her past. When she felt lonely, instead of sitting at home stewing about it, she would visit someone. If she was feeling unappreciated or 'forgotten', she would pick a flower or buy a chocolate and give it to someone who looked like they needed cheering-up – often a complete stranger she'd met on the street or at the shops. When she found herself becoming overly focused on what she thought she was missing out on, she would think of creative ways to meet someone else's needs. She began to feel more positive about herself and about life in general. She continued to walk, to give, and to participate in life. She is a whole new creation.

There was a time when Mel was difficult to be with, when she was lost in self-pity, deep hurts and resentments. Now, she is much softer and 'lighter', if you know what I mean, and there is a sense of peace and contentment that is growing and blossoming from within. She is grateful for every gift, every visit, and every experience of life now. I have known her for about fifteen years, and I'm always tickled pink whenever I see her these days. I should mention that she has recently completed a mathematics degree as well, and studied while serving in Mozambique with Heidi Baker ministries for two months – how's that for a 'nothing's going to hold me down' attitude! The transformation within her is nothing short of miraculous, and it all began with a simple decision to take her eyes off of herself, and to begin to see the needs of others.

Psychologists, counsellors and mental-health workers all agree that one of the most significant activities that impacts long-term happiness is the simple act of showing kindness. Those who habitually help others, with no thought of reward for themselves, score much higher in 'happiness assessments'. In a similar way, grateful people typically have a better sense of belonging and lower levels of depression and stress than those who are ungrateful. Happiness is actually quite a paradox. If you seek it directly for yourself without consideration for the wellbeing and happiness of others, you won't ever find it, but if you look to make others happy, it often comes to you as a by-product of living well; of being 'other-centred'.

One time when we were down in Victoria we got involved in a project with the Planet Shakers Church in Fitzroy, Melbourne. It had come to their attention that some of the high density, multi-storeyed government-housing blocks were in dire need of a good clean-up. The plan was to go into these buildings with large teams of volunteers and scrub down the walls and ceilings, especially targeting the abundance of offensive graffiti. It was a great day, with laughter and happy chatter ringing throughout the buildings. We worked hard in chilly conditions but the sense of satisfaction was priceless. Afterwards, the various clean-up teams and a number of happy residents joined together for a big BBQ lunch (free to the residents of course) in one of the outdoor areas. There were so many smiling faces at that barbecue you would have thought it was Christmas.

Over the past decade or more, my hubby and I have participated in group planned days of 'Random Acts of Kindness', a bit of an oxymoron there. But the principal has been that you volunteer your time and set out to make people feel happy, no strings attached; no payback. We've never had so much fun. One example was giving out bottles of water to stressed-looking shoppers with teams of people from Highway Christian Church in Ulladulla NSW in the heat of summer. People were so grateful – and it put a smile on their dial which transferred to a smile on our faces.

At my youngest son's church, C3 in Oxford Falls NSW, they have specially-designed stickers (by my clever daughter-in-love) that say 'Kindness for Goodness Sake'. I love the philosophy of everyone feeling encouraged to remember the importance of being other-centred, and to inspire creative ways to be randomly kind to people and simply share love, joy and happy vibes.

We were in Port Macquarie for a convention and met a young girl working in a bar one evening. We were the only people in the bar at the time, and she just started telling us some of the dilemmas she was trying to sort through in her head. She was attempting to figure out what she needed to keep, and what she should throw away in her life. She told a familiar tale of how she had been hurt by 'the church'. Unfortunately many people get so sick to death of religion that they actually throw God away in their confusion and frustration. It's like chucking out the baby with the bath water. Because of the hurts she had experienced, she had been distancing herself from God and missing out on the pure, liberating love she needed. As we built her up and encouraged her, we watched her face change. A huge grin spread across her face as she realised she didn't have to live up to any ridiculous 'religious' standards any more, only allow God to love her and show her the best way forward. I tell you, the REAL Gospel message is something people are LONGING to hear.

CHAPTER NINETEEN
good grief

The Old Testament book, Nehemiah, has a verse I'm especially fond of, 'the joy of the Lord is your strength'. It's a verse that's often thrown about in Christian circles, and is one that is particularly relevant when things aren't going your way or you're not quite feeling the love, joy and happy vibes. The rationale behind it is to remind ourselves who God is, especially in the midst of our trials and hardships, and to remember who we are - God's chosen people, his very own children who he dearly loves. If we focus on this truth, rather than on our immediate problems, we can rise above our difficulties and be sustained by the supernatural joy and strength that God provides. Hands up who wouldn't like supernatural strength to get through the tough times of life? Der... it's a bit of a no-brainer wouldn't you agree? We can struggle through our circumstances, we can wallow in our circumstances, or we can do the seemingly crazy, totally irrational thing, and praise God in spite of our circumstances. If we choose to do the latter, our circumstances will no longer determine whether we are happy or not, and a whole new reality will open up for us.

Trusting God when it feels like everything is going wrong doesn't necessarily come naturally or easily, and our first response can still be to whinge, swear, and kick the cat (I haven't got one, but I'd like to think I might if I did have one). Fortunately I usually come to my senses pretty quickly these days, and I try to keep things in perspective and tap into what I've learnt over the last thirty years about God's faithfulness and goodness. Keep in mind that it has taken me many years to get to that place, so don't be too uptight if you feel you can't trust God too much just yet. Like all good, healthy relationships, it takes time to get to know and trust the other person, and it's usually no different with God.

Often, it is *in spite* of circumstances that people rise, and *because of* circumstances that people choose to pursue a life of value and purpose. And here is Nehemiah telling us we don't need to be sad, discouraged or feel dejected - we can find strength even in the most trying circumstances by trusting in the goodness and faithfulness of God. And let me tell you, Nehemiah was no stranger to trouble and hardship. He worked with his tools of trade in one hand, and a sword in the other because he lived with the fear of being attacked and killed by his enemies, at any time. In the midst of the most challenging circumstances, Nehemiah chose joy, and because of that choice, he was given the strength to endure and rise above those circumstances.

Ah, a perfect opportunity for one of my quirky sayings here, 'I don't sing because I'm happy, I'm happy because I sing'. If we choose to, we can actually create much of our own happiness, and once we understand our potential to do this, we have a formidable tool or weapon at our disposal. Keep in mind though that there are times when feeling sad or down is completely appropriate, and may even be beneficial for us. Being sad or feeling down can move us to think about and contemplate the deeper, more meaningful aspects of life, and as such can be potent catalysts for change. Moods and feelings that we tend to regard and classify as 'negatives', are actually an integral part of the human experience, and it's usually only when we get *stuck* in them that they become unproductive, or even destructive.

By way of explanation let me tell you about some grief counselling I received shortly after my dad's death. This proved to be a valuable healing time for me and the family, and the clarity and balance it provided has enabled us to help many others through their grieving. Actually, I think it would be wise to teach our children about grieving and loss at school, especially when you consider the fact that we all sooner or later have to face the reality of loss and death. Maybe some healthy, good education on the subject could go a long way to preventing unnecessary or prolonged pain and suffering – just a thought. I know I could have done with it years before, as I think a lot of my earlier life was spent grieving. There are no rules or clearly-defined time-lines for grieving – which means no rights and no wrongs. Tony, a friend of mine who has known much loss, once told me, 'It's not about grief management, it's about grief awareness'.

While the grief process may be broken down into five different stages, the order, duration, and intensity of these stages can vary enormously. The stages include *denial, anger, bargaining, depression* and *acceptance*. The rate at which people move through these stages varies enormously though, and there are no hard and fast rules or set time-frames when it comes to transitioning from one to the other. We are all wired so differently that it would be ludicrous to expect our thoughts and feelings to follow some clearly-defined, predetermined pathway through grief. When we lose someone or something that is near and dear to us, it generally rocks our world and shakes things at a foundational level, and so we need time to process the experience and adjust ourselves to our 'new' state of being - similar to before, but never quite the same. Where people haven't the resources or support they need to deal with the experience, they may become stuck in one of the stages - denial, anger, or depression for example.

Because there can be so many raw emotions spilling over with grief, it's important to have a few good, mature people around so that you have 'permission' to grieve properly and 'get things off your chest' as stuff arises. I'm no expert, but I think one of the main reasons that people get stuck in grief is holding back emotionally, suppressing how they're really feeling instead of letting it all hang out. *Good listeners* are worth their weight in gold in grief situations, so find one when you need one, and be one for your family and friends when they need one.

In my experience (and of those I've been privileged to journey with) once we've allowed ourselves the time we need to grieve properly, and once we've arrived at a place of acceptance (however uncomfortable that feels), we can start to look outward and enter the world proper once again. The gaping wound begins to heal, but a scar still remains. I'm OK with that. Scars remind us of our humanity, our frailty, and ultimately, our mortality! I'm learning to look to God as my dependable supply of strength and power, and to remember that even if I feel alone, God is there to provide the comfort and strength I need. And let's not forget that tiny little flower, pushing up through the dirt, spreading its petals towards the sunshine.

Just as we can't avoid having to grieve at some stage in life, we can't avoid pain. I used to think that if I had a pain-free life I'd be happy. But there's no such thing. I've learnt that pain can be a great teacher. When I was helping hubby build a planter box so we could grow some vegies and herbs, I happened to hit my thumb with the hammer, which resulted in a very clear warning signal being sent to every part of my body. I knew instantly that something was wrong, and I knew that to continue hitting my thumb with the hammer was only going to produce the same result or worse... and I knew that my husband would quite competently finish building the planter box without any further assistance from his thumb-sucking wife.

Nehemiah's secret is that he sought God. We can do the same. We can ask God to spark our imaginations, to strengthen our resolve, to open the right doors, to keep our attitude right and to provide what we need to get the job done – how cool is that? Failures usually come when we depend too much on our own strength. God is always waiting for his kids to ask. The bible portrays God as an attentive father, sitting on the edge of his seat, leaning forward, watching our progress and excited to hear our requests. He can't wait to give us dreams and plans to run with, and he can't wait to provide the means to make them happen – he's just waiting for the invite.

I began the process of defining my purpose and building vision by sitting down with a couple of close friends and family members, and you can too. Don't just ask anyone though, make sure it's people who know you well and who love you, and whose opinions you can respect. Ask them what gifts and talents they think you have, or if your self-esteem can cope with it, you might ask them to help you list your strengths and weaknesses (like I did in Newcastle that day with my hubby and son). In Romans 12:6-8, it says, 'In his grace, God has given us different gifts for doing certain things well. So if God has given you the gift to serve others, serve them well. If you are a teacher, teach well. If your gift is to encourage others, be encouraging. If it's giving, give generously. If God has given you leadership ability, take the responsibility seriously. And if you have a gift for showing kindness to others, do it gladly.'

Spend time thinking it over if you need to. Don't rush the process; it's too important for that. Remember, life is a marathon, not a sprint. My hubby and I took years to put together a vision for our life. We used to sit and dream and chat and hope and pray and imagine. We found that writing things down helped us clarify the vision, and it gave us something to kick us off at the next dreaming session. In between times, we would maintain a healthy diet of inspirational books – a bit like the one you're reading now – to keep us motivated and expectant. So congratulations, you're off to a brilliant start.

Don't get so caught-up in achieving your goals that you forget to enjoy the journey. Think holistically and take in all aspects of your life - spiritual, financial, emotional, mental and physical. Why not have goals that feed health and wholeness into all areas. And don't forget the overriding importance of enjoying the journey or the process, not just at the end, because 'now' is really all we ever have to work with. As Kahlil Gibran said, 'Yesterday is gone forever, and tomorrow is yet a dream; today is the very life of life.'

One time as we were leisurely making our way from NSW down to Victoria, we encountered the nastiest mosquitoes (or 'mozziemites' as our 3-year-old granddaughter says) we'd ever come across. We had a belly full of pizza from a dinner stop at Bairnsdale, the sun was sinking fast, and we were too tired to keep driving. We kept waiting to find a nice, appealing rest-stop along the road, but we found none. So we decided the next place we came across would have to do. We drove into a quiet little town called Rosedale and noticed a park off the highway to our right called The Willows (I still break out into a cold sweat with the mention of that place). We pulled into the park, jumped out of Buzz and prepared to set up for the night. Before we knew what hit us we were repeatedly and viciously attacked by what can only be described as swarms of Killer Mozzies. We realised, far too late to do anything about it, that we had inadvertently gate-crashed a Regional Mosquito Convention. These blood-thirsty mothers were not your average breed, no, there was also an unusually high percentage of kamikaze mozzies amongst them, the type that push themselves so hard against the insect screens covering your windows that they either squeeze their way through the tiny holes to get to you, or kill themselves in the process. Whether it was sleep deprivation, blood loss, or a genuine epiphany, I'm still not sure, but I could have sworn I saw tiny little navy singlets on some of those guys, and overheard a bunch of them bragging about who could down the most schooners of 'Aerogard'.

After a long, noisy, sleepless, swatting, sweaty night, we were very thankful to see the sun finally coming up. The inside of our van reminded me of the beach-landing scene from the movie, 'Saving Private Ryan' - there was blood and squished mozzies everywhere. Just as we were about to hightail it out of that mosquito-infested cesspool, a fellow traveller wandered over for a chat. It wasn't long before Daryl started to pour his heart out to us. He had suffered two broken marriages and lived with the notion that God was some mean, cane-wielding sadist, eager to punish people at the first opportunity. It became clear that his misconceptions had been 'inherited' from his religious father, who Daryl said, 'had ruled with the big book in one hand and a strap in the other'. It was exciting to introduce him to the real God; the all-loving, all-forgiving father. I get such a kick out of helping people bust out of their wrong mindsets. Having the opportunity to share the truth about God and his unconditional love with Daryl was worth losing half my blood to those wretched mozzies.

One of the greatest stories to illustrate the love God has for us, is found in Luke 15, precisely where we began with Daryl. Yes, it is the story of the prodigal son I mentioned earlier... and who better to tell the tale than Jesus himself. Jesus tells the story of a son who wants his inheritance – which, by the way, he isn't entitled to until his father dies, but this guy wants it now; he isn't prepared to wait. His father decides to let him have it even though it is culturally inappropriate and a shameful thing for the son to do. The son gets his money and takes off. He not only leaves his father's house, but he makes sure he gets as far away as he can. He heads to a faraway country where he parties hard until all his money is spent. To cut a long story short, now he's broke. He's living in a foreign country and has no family to support him through the tough times. A famine hits the place where he's living, and work is hard to find. He lands a job tending pigs for a farmer, but his earnings are so pitiful and his situation so desperate that he even becomes envious of the pigs and the food they're eating. He eventually comes to his senses and realises that even his father's servants are living much better than he is. He decides that he will go back home, beg his father's forgiveness, and see if he can work as one of his father's servants. It's a long journey home, mostly on foot or occasionally hitching a ride, until finally he gets within view of his father's property. You can imagine what he's thinking, 'I've disgraced myself. I've disgraced my father and the family name. I've blown my inheritance and now there's nothing left to look forward to. I am a loser with a capital L, AND, I can expect to get the cold-shoulder from my father.'

Meanwhile, unbeknown to the son, his father has been hoping against all hope that his boy will one day come home. As his father goes about his daily business on the family property, he compulsively searches the surrounding country-side for any sign of his dear son coming back to him. Even though he knows it's unlikely, he never gives up looking, and hoping, and waiting. The story goes on to say that while the son was still a long way off, the father, who had been eagerly watching for his return, sees him and runs to meet him. The father is full of love and compassion for his son, and when he gets to him he throws his arms around him and kisses him. The son is overwhelmed and begs his father for forgiveness and the chance to work as a servant. The father calls to his servants and tells them to get a robe for his son, and a ring to put on his finger (both are signs of authority and family-standing). He tells them to make preparations for a feast so they can celebrate his return. The story finishes with the father's heart-felt explanation of why a celebration was in order, 'This son of mine was dead but has come back to life; he was lost and now is found.'

Jesus told this story so that we could understand the heart of our heavenly father. He knew better than anyone how far our concept of God had strayed from the truth, so he made it a priority to reveal what the father was really like, and to have us know what sort of reception we could expect if we decided to 'come home to him'. This is one of my all-time favourite bible stories because it dispels any misconceptions about God being hard and unforgiving. Be assured that he is just like Jesus portrays him to be in this story, and just like King David found him to be, even after committing murder and adultery - 'merciful and gracious, slow to get angry and full of unfailing love'.

Daryl isn't the only one who has needed to hear the truth about God's love, and we'd be hard pressed to recall the number of times we've been able to relate this story to others on our journey. I love that the prodigal's father immediately drops what he's doing and RUNS. He runs to his child, not to scold him or to judge him, not to say 'I told you so' or to shame him, not to humiliate or condemn him. No, he runs to his child to EMBRACE him. That's God's heart for you. No matter how bad your past has been, God promises to give you a fresh start; a clean slate! God actually says that he will 'remember your past no more' - how cool is that! He's got plans for you, plans for good, plans to prosper you, plans to give you hope, plans to usher you into a fantastic future. That's Jeremiah 29:11 – a popular verse in Christian circles, for obvious reasons. After sharing this with Daryl we had the pleasure of watching the lights go on for him, and as we parted ways we noticed something had tangibly changed in his eyes. Ah, no greater joy!

* * *

One night before we even took off in Buzz, I invited a stranger home to have dinner with us (this wasn't all that unusual for me I might add). I was working for the local newspaper and was out and about taking photographs, when I noticed this guy. He was sitting in his car alone when I walked past, and was still there as I was returning to the office some time later. He waved me over and we got chatting. He told me he was in the area for work and that he had been staying in a motel for quite some time. He told me he was missing his wife and children terribly, so I gave him my address and a few hours later he arrived on our doorstep. Dinner at our house that night was one of the loudest, craziest times we've had. Most of our children were there, together with a couple of their friends, and this stranger, all sharing one of my hubby's infamous curries that he whips up so easily. It was a hoot. Our guest kept shaking his head in wonder, and saying how great it felt to be at a dinner table with 'family' again. After a month of living out of motels and eating alone he marvelled at the simple joys of being able to share a meal with us. Turns out our stranger had landed a big work contract in our local area and was looking for people to work for him, and my youngest son just happened to be in need of employment. Voila, the two clicked that night and my son went to work for him a few days later, AND, he had stable employment for the next 12 months until the contract finished! Crazy the stuff God does when we're open to him, eh.

I met an old man on the beach. Well, I hadn't really 'met' him, and he wasn't as old as I first thought. Let me explain. This man and I walked the same beach, at the same time, pretty much every day, and as he walked past me I noticed he was badly hunched over, and always seemed to have a cranky look on his face. We passed one another for a number of weeks before I finally approached him and introduced myself (since first seeing him I'd been praying for him and doing the usual 'good morning' nod of the head, but hadn't felt to actually stop and talk). So this particular morning I stopped, and after introducing myself, I wrapped my arms around him and gave him a big hug. I've always been a huggy person, so it just came naturally (I'm so used to hugging that I get shocked when others get shocked at me hugging them – if you know what I mean). When I looked into his eyes, he had tears escaping down his cheeks. He explained to me that he had lost his wife many years before, and since then nobody ever hugged him. I love that I was put on that beach, at that time, to hug that man. Before hubby and I left town to travel on in Buzz, my beach buddy and I saw each other almost every day, and when he saw me approaching he would straighten his Parkinson's-affected body, and await my hug. It was beautiful. And yes, he too was invited home to share one of Step's gourmet meals, and as a bonus he got to experience the fun, laughter and mayhem which characterises our family gatherings.

CHAPTER TWENTY
good for a city

Have you heard of Charles Darrow? No, neither had I. Darrow was a heater salesman until he lost his job in 1929. He could have sat around feeling sorry for himself, but instead he decided to put his mind and talents to good use developing a board-game, first on oil cloth, then cardboard. He took it to Parker Bros and Milton Bradley, and guess what? They rejected it. Poor Charles; all those years of designing and planning, and it all went down the gurgler... or did it? In 1934, Parker Bros had a change of mind, and voila, Darrow soon became a millionaire from the sales of his board game, Monopoly. In 1936 alone, 20,000 Monopoly games were sold - every week! The rest is history. Charles Darrow's *failure* as a heater salesman was what propelled him into an unknown, yet incredibly successful future. He had vision, believed in his dream, and he followed through with it - in spite of the setbacks.

Few of us would expect to achieve success on the same scale as good ol' Charlie Darrow did. He became a millionaire from it (very nice bonus there) and some of us still play his game! Oh, I don't mean we are still playing the *same* game – though my sons had a game going for nine days during one school holiday period. I was amazed... usually the board got tipped over in disgust by the end of day one. My eldest son had a habit of claiming every set and buying houses and motels until his sibling opponents quivered in fear every time they had to roll the dice.

But Darrow's millions and my eldest son's monopoly on Monopoly aren't the point. We each have something unique to offer the world, and it's up to us to get off our bums and have a go. It's not about whether we fail or not, and it's certainly not about making millions of dollars (even though I'm sure I'd be OK with that), it's really about 'giving it a crack' as my friend Graeme likes to say; having a go. Some of us are so hung-up and paranoid about the possibility of failure that we hide in our shell and never risk anything. That's what I call true failure – giving up before you've even had a decent 'crack' at it.

I'm not trying to be morbid here, but even if I died right now, I would die a happy woman. I love my life – all of it - the good, the bad, and the ugly. I have had the most amazing time here on planet earth, and in spite of my many failures, I have no regrets. Sure, I've done my fair share of dumb things and hurtful things (who hasn't), but because of God's grace I have been forgiven and released from lugging these things around with me. In Hebrews chapter eight, the bible says that when we accept what Jesus has done for us, we can come to God and he will, 'never again remember our sins.' If God chooses to leave my past failures in the past, who am I to keep beating myself up over them!

I've been loved and supported by many beautiful people along life's way, and I've been blessed to have been used to help others along their way. I feel content and fulfilled, and to tell you the truth, I can't think of a single person I would rather be. That may sound bizarre in light of my past struggles, or a little uppity, but it's true. I love being me. Hubby and I often climb into Buzz after social events or gatherings, and say to one another, 'I'm so glad we're us.' We really are happy with our simple life. My hubby often reminds me that the simple, uncomplicated life still beats almost anything else hands down. We feel very privileged to have each other, our family and our friends, and we relish the opportunities we have in meeting new 'friends' along the way.

In the book of Proverbs (11:11) it says, 'Upright citizens are good for a city and make it prosper, but the talk of the wicked tears it apart.' Each and every one of us has the potential to make a difference in our town or city - for good or for bad. My hubby and I are certainly no super-heroes, and we are keenly aware that there are plenty of people out there doing much more than we ever could to make the world a better place. But in spite of all that, we know we have been called to this little part of the world to make a difference - even if it is only in a small way - and we love the challenge of it. We enjoy trying to focus on what we can do and on what we have to offer, not on the things we are powerless to change. We understand the principal of sowing and reaping, that we're not only blessing others as we go about trying to do good, but we're also investing in our own lives, and our own future. Such a crazy concept, that little ol' you and little ol' me can help change a city. 'Upright citizens are good for a city and make it prosper, but the talk of the wicked tears it apart.' The second part of this proverb gives us a stern warning about the destructive power of negative words. Things like gossip, criticism, slander and lies can literally tear relationships and communities apart (that is pretty heavy stuff); we need to be on guard against them.

My life is filled with positive thinking and happy vibes these days, vibes I try to share with others, wherever we are. I don't have all the answers to life – I'm just a gal who loves life and gets a kick out of encouraging others to do the same. The happy vibes only come about as a result of the choices I make; they don't just happen automatically because I want them to. It's the same with negative thinking, unforgiveness, resentment, envy, jealousy, and the bad vibes that they generate; they're a choice. If you want good vibes to come your way, you really need to stop and consider what vibes you yourself are putting out.

It's a medically-proven fact that people's health can be adversely affected by negative thought patterns and negative emotional states. Do you really want to increase your risk of developing conditions like irritable-bowel syndrome, arthritis, hypertension, depression, heart-disease and cancer? We need to keep in mind that there are consequences for everything. God himself has declared that a person will always reap what they sow (it keeps coming back to that, eh) - good or bad. If our motivation in life is love - for others and for ourselves - we can't really go wrong. Love has been God's motivation from the beginning of time, and if we want the 'good life' for ourselves, love should be our motivation too. When we stop striving for more; when we accept that peace and happiness can't be found in material things, or through living a self-indulgent life; when we earnestly desire to be the best we can be and to live in harmony with others; then we will begin to 'blossom where we are planted', and hopefully, 'be good for a city and make it prosper.'

You and I have the power to change our own lives and the lives of those around us in our towns and cities when we live with purpose and passion – with vision. Proverbs 29:18 reminds us that 'without a vision people perish.' Do you know another word for perish? DIE! Wow - without vision, people die! We were created to have something to live for, something to strive for and work towards. Without knowing our purpose, how can we expect to take a proper hold of life? And if we don't take a proper hold of life, there's every chance that we'll miss out on experiencing the fullness and satisfaction that was meant for us.

So then, if you really want to live, I invite you to ask for help. I know I couldn't have made it this far without God's help; I would've been dead – literally! I certainly wouldn't be here writing this book without him. He was (and is) my hope, my help, and my inspiration. I'm convinced that God can help you see the bigger picture, and only God can give you the drive, energy and passion to fulfil the purpose you were created for.

I've seen so many false-starts and disqualifications from people who've had a seemingly healthy desire to rise and do something significant, but they weren't prepared to humble themselves and call on God for help. I reckon it's impossible without his help. You can go so far, but in the end it counts for nothing. It breaks my heart to see people, full of potential and purpose, struggling on alone when the whole time God is right there, waiting for them to ask for his help. Whatever your current situation: broken and desperate; struggling but getting by; or even succeeding in your plans and living comfortably; God can bring change to your world and cause you to prosper in ways you couldn't even imagine. All we have to do is humble ourselves and ask. The bible tells us that, God opposes the proud, but gives grace to the humble. That's a tough decision isn't it – Do I want opposition from God, or grace from God? Hhmm, now let me think...

Still, one of the biggest issues we have to confront and overcome before we can comfortably call on God to help, is the issue of trust. It's all good and well to say that God loves us and is on our side, but if we don't KNOW him, how can we trust him? One day when Jesus was hanging out with his disciples they said to him, 'Jesus, there's one thing we really want to know, and that is, what does the father (that's God) look like?' What they were saying was, 'We really want to see him for ourselves so that we can know, once and for all, whether he is trustworthy like you say he is.' I love Jesus' reply. He said, 'Don't you know me by now? The father and I are one and the same. Now that you've seen me, you've seen the father.' When we look at the life of Jesus we see God himself in action – reaching out to the poor, the broken, the marginalised, the down-trodden, the hurting and the sick, and we see nothing but love, grace and forgiveness freely poured out to meet every need. And then, just in case there were any lingering doubts, Jesus paid the ultimate price, dying a torturous death nailed to a cross, so that you and I would never have to fear God or run from him.

The bible makes it clear that sin is the thing that separates us from God, and that Jesus died on our behalf to pay the penalty for our sin. It also teaches that apart from him, there is no other way that we can make peace with God and become his friends. If we trust in Jesus and his sacrifice, we have a guarantee that we will never be rejected or turned away, no matter what! If we choose to ignore such an extravagant display of God's love however, we will have to 'face the music' for all of our sins and failings, and pay the penalty ourselves. The book of Romans makes it plain and clear that 'the wages of sin is death, but the free gift of God is eternal life through Jesus Christ.' This 'free gift' is yours for the taking, but know this: it is not yours and never will be yours unless you personally ask for it. You don't receive it when you're christened or baptised as a baby; it isn't automatically yours because your family always went to church; and you don't get it because you're a 'nice' person. The bible says that ALL sin and fall short of God's standard – that's me, and whether you like it or not, that's you. The only way to receive this 'free gift' is to humble ourselves and ask for it.

Start by being thankful for whatever good things you've got going on (Elaine would be hurriedly grabbing her purple pen and a clean sheet of purple paper right now, and be pumping out one of her infamous mega-lists: life, family, talents, work, home, friends, health). Ask for eyes to see all the good things you've been given. God loves you and thinks the world of you. As a matter of fact he loves you so much, he couldn't live without you. 'I love you this much,' he said, and he stretched his arms wide upon that cross and sacrificed his life for yours. So if you've never done it before, why don't you thank Jesus for all he has done on your behalf, and ask him to help you live the life he intended for you to live? Why not do it now? This can be the most significant day of your life. This 'simple' decision opens the door for incredible blessings, benefits, and the favour of God to be on your life - starting now, and stretching into eternity!

If you did decide to take this momentous step, let me be the first to CONGRATULATE you. WOOHOO! The bible says that you are now BORN AGAIN – which is referring to your spirit: that part of you that 'once was dead in sin, but now is alive in Christ.' Your slate has literally been wiped clean - just as if you never did anything wrong - and your destiny is forever linked to God. You're a part of his family now - a totally forgiven, fully accepted, deeply loved, daily empowered child of God ha-ha, how cool is that? And he is absolutely committed to growing you as a person, and will be your greatest supporter for the rest of your life and beyond.

You'll recall the welcome and honour the prodigal son received when he came home to his father's outstretched arms? That's exactly what *you* can expect. And even though he knows every messy detail of your past, he puts it all behind you and gives you a fresh start. 'For I know the plans I have for you (insert your name here)' says the Lord. 'They are plans to prosper you and not to harm you, plans to give you a future and a hope.' 'When you pray, I will listen. If you look for me wholeheartedly, you will find me... I will end your captivity and restore your fortunes.' Jeremiah 29:11-14. Take heart, the God of the universe is on YOUR side. What more could you need; what more could you possibly hope for?

CHAPTER TWENTY ONE
crappy beginnings

Do you know how the Kleenex tissue came about? No? Well, allow me to enlighten you. Kimberly Clark was a paper manufacturer in 1924. Part of his business was in manufacturing women's pads using crepe paper, but unfortunately sales were slow. Women weren't too sure about using disposable pads in those days. Clark had already manufactured the paper, so he had to work out what he would do with it all. Instead of sulking or quitting (which one could almost excuse), he put together a team to work on the project, and later released it back on the market as a cold-cream remover (in those days women had a towel that hung near their basins for removing makeup, but it was typically dirty and unsightly). One day in 1930, one of his staff, who was having trouble with hay-fever, grabbed a 'cold cream remover' instead of her handkerchief, and proceeded to blow her nose. And thus, the Kleenex tissue was born.

So there you have it - the original plan for the Kleenex tissue was to be used at the other end of a woman's anatomy. And note this - Kimberly Clark's products are now used by more than a billion people every day. I guess this story reminds us that adversity can be a blessing in disguise, so don't ever let a crappy beginning rob you of a magnificent ending.

I was employed as a journalist over a ten year period, for three different rural newspapers mind you, without ever undergoing any formal journalistic training. And I worked as a personal secretary without ever completing my TAFE secretarial course. I'm not sure what message this is sending you, but I do want to emphasise that if God wants you in a certain place it doesn't matter what qualifications you have or don't have – he can make a way even when there seems to be no way! Please, don't give up because your beginning was lousy.

I'm so glad that we aren't defined by what we do or don't do, aren't you? Unfortunately for me, I spent the first 20 years of my life thinking I was a loser, so you can well understand why I have so little tolerance for that kind of thinking in my life now. I've wasted enough time wallowing in the mud. My failures, hardships, mistakes, losses and pain, have only added character and colour to me... and what a rainbow of colour it is! I know the talents and gifts that have been given to me, and it's up to me to put them to good use. I want to use them to make a difference, to add value to the lives of others. Do you know that God plans for you to make a difference too? You can love who you are and you can love what you do.

You can make your own life great, and you can help other people make their life worth living. That's something to aspire to, don't you think?

As you know, I attempted to take my life (but God intervened); I had an emotional breakdown (and God used it to make me a stronger person); and my marriage had all but fallen apart (and God used that crisis to help us appreciate our differences). I can't afford to let setbacks get me down or hold me back. I've tried it my way and discovered one very important factor: our hope and confidence are in God. Now, I know I'm pretty good, but I'm not great. I'm a fantastic mother to my five children and a groovy granny, but I'm not much without God behind me. It's God who has seen me through my dark and painful experiences, and it is because of him that I am who I am today.

Hubby loves study. Somehow I think I'm not cut out for all those theories, protocols and hypotheses – I'm convinced that too much structured learning would only rob me of my individuality and creativity (well that's my story and I'm sticking to it). Anyway, I like to keep it real, and funnily enough I often have people use that term after hearing me speak in public. 'I love that you're so real about everything', they say. Maybe if I had a few 'tickets' to my name I wouldn't be quite so down to earth (being boastful *is* a sanguine failing after all). Anyway, one of my sayings is, 'If you can't be perfect, attach yourself to someone who is.' That's why I'm with my hubby. He has lots of qualifications, both formal and informal, and he seems to have been given enough sticking power for both of us. If I need something explained I can usually go to him. Even my five-year-old granddaughter has noticed how it works between us, as just yesterday I heard her say, 'Pa has to do *everything* for Granny.' God bless her little cotton socks. By the way, she is the same grandchild who recently asked me how to spell 'tired' while we were doing craft activities together. With her little head bent down to her work she scribbled away until she looked up and handed me a card. 'I love you Granny, you are the best Granny in the whole in tired world.' My heart melted.

I want you right now to sit back for a few quiet moments. Allow your mind to wonder (that's wonder, not wander) why you are the way you are, why you think and do things as you do. Now ask God to show you any hidden gifts and talents that you may not be aware of yet - ask him what he sees when he looks at you. That's powerful stuff right there, powerful enough to change your life forever.

Be ready to receive answers to your questions. Answers can come in so many different ways it's almost impossible to pre-empt how they will come – just be excited and be expectant. God loves to move on many different levels, so when he gets involved, look out, absolutely anything is possible (the options are truly limitless). Once you've received the inspiration you need to 'see' your life's purpose, vision should naturally start to rise. Once vision becomes clearly defined it acts like a road map or GPS to keep you heading in the right direction. After that, feed it, nurture it, and maybe tweak it a little as you go. The next step I'd recommend is to write yourself a mission statement - your reason for being alive. Plaster it around where you live so that you can't get away from it (whip out those post-it-notes again). Make a point of reading it every day, and when you do, read it OUT LOUD!!

A dream written down with a date becomes a goal; a goal broken down into steps becomes a plan; and a plan backed by consistent action makes dreams come true. OK, let's think about that... start by writing down something that you're passionate about, something that gets you pumped up and energised. Now think of what you would like to do in this particular field or area – maybe a need or a gap that you could potentially fill. Keep it positive, as negative or subversive ideas won't attract the kind of backing, support and energy you'll need to succeed. Now break your goals down into small, specific, realistically-achievable steps (take your time, don't rush the process). Once you've done that, set *realistic time-frames or dead-lines* for starting and completing each and every one of the steps. Now you've got your plan, all you have to do is stick to it – no matter what!

And whatever you do, make sure it's YOUR vision. You simply won't have the drive and perseverance you need if it isn't your own vision. Do what you do well, and let others do what they do well! Live in your 'space', and allow others to live in their 'space', AND, have respect for our differences. Before I liked who I was, I would occasionally meet someone really cool and attempt to imitate them for a time... until I got tired of trying and failing. It was a big enough challenge being me, let alone trying to be someone else. I soon discovered that trying to copy someone else's habits and behaviour didn't work because it was only focusing on the outward things. More important by far is what's happening on the inside of a person, because that is what really dictates what we see on the outside. Once I opened up and invited God to do a work in me - from the inside out - I began to find my real self (I'd been hiding under a blanket of fear, rejection and hurt for years), and with his help I've been able to continue to move towards being the person I was created to be. And the journey certainly isn't over; not by a long shot.

Don't forget there may be some practical things to do - like training, study, or practise – whatever you need to do to keep moving towards achieving your goals and dreams. Remember, proper planning and preparation produce productivity (I think I just made that up). If it all sounds a bit scary, know that you're not alone, and that almost everyone encounters fear and apprehension when stepping out into something new. I read once, 'you may succeed if nobody else believes in you, but will never succeed if you don't believe in yourself.' The key is to be honest with yourself about what your capabilities are (and aren't!), and above all, DON'T PANIC!

And as I mentioned earlier, it's the journey that's most important, not the arriving. It's during the journey that we are challenged to change and grow; it's where we develop perseverance, self-discipline, discernment, tolerance, compassion, people skills, and all those other qualities that define real maturity. Because we are all travellers on a journey through this life and into the next, none of us ever fully 'arrive' in the truest sense of the word, so to spend our life pursuing goals and dreams without making an effort to enjoy the journey is pretty dumb when you think about it. Those people that suffer from 'get-there-disease' think they can't be happy until they've achieved all they want. Some people forget that they are actually living while they are planning to live, and are so busy planning to live, that they never live at all. What a tragedy! They think that arriving at a certain 'destination' will automatically bring them happiness, and yet nothing could be further from the truth.

Now, don't get me wrong, it's great to have determination and focus if you want to achieve goals, in fact, it's essential. The problem is when we become fixated on something off in the future it can be at the expense of the 'here and now'. You can miss so much of life. Remember that. When we first set goals, we can be all gung-ho about them and just want to 'get there' but the plan is to keep one eye on the 'prize', and one eye on wherever you're at right now. Don't sacrifice today's joy for tomorrow's dream, and by the same token, don't sacrifice tomorrow's dream by living only for the joys of today. It's quite a balancing act at times!

Another saying I'm fond of is, 'We conquer by continuing.' It sounds too simple to be true, yet a large component of any success is due to perseverance - keeping on and keeping going. My friend Graeme is learning guitar. He has wanted to play guitar for many years. Recently, he actually decided to do something about it. He bought new strings for his guitar, bought some sheet-music, and booked in for lessons. The quantum leap from 'wanting to play', to 'doing something about it', made all the difference. Mohammad Ali (the first and only three-time world heavyweight boxing champion) says it best, 'Champions aren't made in the gyms, they are made from something deep inside them – a desire, a dream, a vision. They have last-minute stamina. They have to be a little faster, and they have to have the skill and the will. But the will must be stronger than the skill.'

Graeme no longer has to wonder what could have been or what might have been. Now he's not only playing guitar (and loving it), but he is also pursuing other dreams that he had put in the too-hard basket. I think 'Nike' got it right with their hugely successful advertising campaign from yesteryear, 'Just Do It!' And then, once you've done it, just keep on doing it for as long as it takes!

Have I told you about Graeme? Though he is a decade older than me, I'm often a 'mum' to Graeme. He needs me, I tell myself as I pick up his jumper from the floor or remind him his mobile phone is still on the table at the cafe we're about to leave, or return his book he left open on the camp chair the night before. He could very easily be mistaken for the love child of Mr Magoo and Mr Bean, if you know what I mean. He gets into all sorts of fixes that just magically work themselves out, sometimes with him completely oblivious to the wake of destruction that may have been left behind.

Graeme entered our world a couple of years back. We met him in a cafe, actually. One of those random things, where you see one another across the cafe and nod a polite 'hello' but something magical has passed between you, and before you know it, you have joined tables together and are sitting chatting comfortably like long-lost friends. It's weird how that happens. What I like about him most is his laugh. He is the kind of guy who throws his head back and laughs loudly, easily and infectiously. Yet, similar to my delightful hubby, he can be both deeply philosophical and sensitive - a pleasant mix. And these days you can find the two of them sitting; Step with his ukulele and Graeme with his guitar, belting out tunes like 'wannabe' rockstars.

Now, if you're still thinking you ain't got what it takes to make your life a success, don't be discouraged or dismayed; there's always hope. One day Jesus was talking to a religious guy who couldn't get his head around some of the concepts that Jesus was trying to share with him. Jesus reassured him that when it's all said and done, 'humanly speaking it may be impossible, but with God everything is possible.' Those words are for you!

CHAPTER TWENTY TWO
friendship 'L' plates

Recently, an old buddy and I reconnected after many years of having had no contact at all. During the years when our children were little (that's pre high-school), my girlfriend Kay and I were together fairly regularly, probably three or four times a week, as we really enjoyed one another's company. Our children played together often and there wasn't much we didn't know about each other's lives. Kay eventually moved away and spent years travelling about doing missionary work both inside and outside of Australia, and it was during this period that I lost contact with her. For the next ten or fifteen years we didn't hear from one another, and then one day out of the blue I was on Facebook and her daughter recognised my name and got in contact with me. Soon after that Kay and I reunited and were chatting together like it had only been weeks rather than years since we'd spoken. The older I get the more I realise how special friendships like that are, and how they need to be treasured.

I couldn't have survived without some of my gracious girlfriends - my 'sisters-to-other-mothers'. Considering the train-wreck of a person I used to be, I don't know how I got to be so blessed, but I am a living testimony that despite our attempts to sabotage ourselves, God's grace can still rule supreme. My life truly is filled, and I do mean FILLED, with astounding people. As I write about my friends for this book, it appears more like a who's-who column. I hang out with people everyone really ought to know! I mean, they're all self-sacrificing, goal-setting achievers. It is funny, 'cos truth be told, I never actually set out to find people like that – we were simply attracted to one another. And it amazes me even further to think that before I could see any potential within me – they must have. Before I got to the place where I believed I could be someone with goals to pursue and make happen, the friends around me automatically, effortlessly, drew out the best in me. I must have had other people in my life along the way – der obviously – but the ones who have remained dear to my heart are making a significant difference in their sphere of influence. It is in the writing of this book that I realise the full impact of the people I have chosen to keep around me – and I feel privileged to pay tribute to them.

Naturally, I couldn't even begin to list all the significant people who have contributed, sowed, prayed, stayed, and generally supported me through life. Apart from my old, faithful, boarding-school, friend and saviour Karin, and laughter-buddies Elaine, Leann, Dale and Susan, there have been many other soul-sister girlfriends and inspirational men who've stuck by me and championed my life and successes. Fortunately they know who they are, as there really are too many to mention them all individually.

I suppose what I'm trying to emphasise is the importance of having a solid support network around us - being a team player rather than a 'lone-ranger'. We were designed to live and work with other people in community, never in isolation. Many of the mental health issues we face today are a direct result of our culture's failure to make 'community', or meaningful connection with others, a priority. Instead of promoting and fostering the idea of healthy relationships, our culture has tended to do just the opposite, making independence a symbol of success and something to aspire to. I beg to differ. People need people. God made it so - evident since the first chapter of Genesis where God saw that Adam needed a help-mate.

I urge you to think of the people around you who champion you, or could potentially share your days and fill your heart if they were given the opportunity. Of course, your situation will be different from mine, just as the next person's will be different yet again. If you already have a great circle of friends that you love, honour and appreciate, consider yourself very fortunate, and never allow yourself to become complacent about such valuable treasure. If your relationships are pretty crappy, if they're more about what you can get rather than what you can share or give, then they will need some work. A good rule-of-thumb is to remember that you will always reap what you sow. If you want genuine friends who will stick by you through thick n' thin, BE a genuine friend yourself! Sowing and reaping is that universal principle that applies to every facet of life, including relationships (lecture over).

I reckon it is important to position yourself for love: to be loved and to give love. Both are equally important if we want to have a healthy soul life. I used to be a terrible 'friend'... like with Narelle, a very caring, lovable young girl from my primary school days. We were meant to be great buddies but I regularly teased and harassed her until I finally drove her crazy. One day on the way home from school, she snapped and totally lost it. She grabbed me by my hair, which happened to be down to my bum at the time, and dragged me to a telegraph pole, where she proceeded to tie me, by my hair, to said pole. She stormed off and left me humiliated, flailing about helplessly, shouting curses at her, until someone came along and helped untie me from the rough, wooden pole – ripping out chunks of my hair in the process. Looking on the bright side (which I'm more inclined to do these days), it did give a lot of people a good laugh that day, and a great story for those who can picture it in their minds.

And there is Karen, my brother's wife, the one I was holidaying with in Greenpatch when I got a trembling taste of the big blue sea. Many moons ago, when she began dating my brother, she used to dread visiting my parents' home if I was there. I didn't know this until a few years later, but she used to see me as a bully of a person - she being fairly shy by comparison. I had quite a chip on my shoulder and was always trying to prove that I was as good, or better, than the next person. I guess I was a bit jealous of this girl taking my brother's attention and thus would force my opinion upon Karen - and she would cringe, not knowing what to do. I think I was her worst nightmare. Once I allowed God into my life it became obvious that it was crucial to have friendships, so I put in an extra effort, resulting in a great bond with Karen now – we get along like a house on fire. Hubby reckons I still like to argue too much for his liking, but that's only because I'm mostly right ha-ha. Fortunately for me (and everyone else in my life), God helps me see my attitudes and behaviours for what they are – sometimes unacceptable or decidedly unfriendly, so we work on it together, under his gracious, forgiving guidance. And as I share some of my life with you, I hope it encourages you to share yours with others – the good, the bad, the mistakes and the beautiful. If you've been feeling left out, or have tended to isolate yourself from people in the past, then today might just be the day of new beginnings.

Once we discover and appreciate the essential beauty that only friends can bring to our world, we begin trying to be a good friend. I certainly haven't graduated yet, and in some ways I'm still wearing my 'L' plates, but I've got the kind of friends who don't seem to notice how lousy I can be at times, and simply appreciate the encouragement and joy I bring. Or maybe they just make allowance for my many faults and love me anyway. Either way, they've got me covered. I must be doing OK because I don't get tied to telegraph poles any more, and I'm hoping it's not just because my hair is too short to be able to do it. I may seem to be harping on the fact, but I absolutely know I cannot live a fulfilled life without sharing it with others. Once we tap into the power of friendship, we can then extend our hand to help others as we travel along life's way. To love and be loved - isn't that life's purpose?

One very dear new-found friend is a lady who recently moved to our town, and because she wanted to connect with people, she joined a heap of different groups straight up. She spent a couple of months meeting people and testing the waters, and now has a few different groups she loves and attends regularly. She also has a smaller group of friends that she can be more intimate with – of which I am privileged to be one - taking in a movie together, heading to the gym or simply having a D&M over coffee. Even though she is naturally quite a shy person, she managed that in her first six months here. Facebook, Twitter, Instagram, and other social-media networks can also be very handy, particularly if you're interested in rekindling long-lost friendships, like Kay and I did recently. Search your local newspaper for community groups to join. There are gardening groups, view clubs, reading groups or book clubs, writing groups, church, quilting and sewing or bushwalking groups, and sporting clubs. And you can usually find all manner of 12-step groups or miscellaneous courses to get involved in. You just need to make a start and join something, anything, and allow yourself to be knitted together with others.

My passions include dressing in a multitude of coloured and patterned clothing accompanied by mismatched, dangly earrings, one of my infamous mini-skirts and a wrist-full of noisy bracelets. I enjoy the inspiration of dare-devils and eccentric individuals with a never-say-die attitude. Weirdly, I enjoy watching washing dry on a line in the breeze. It calms me. I know 98 per cent of readers are shaking their heads; but the other two percent are nodding 'I know exactly what you mean, Chrissy'. I love the buzz of carnivals, festivals and celebrations (if there isn't one, I'll make one up) - and people are attracted to the freedom I have in being myself. It reflects in the 'sisters' around me. Having moved between different towns and suburbs over the years, together with our travel adventures in Buzz, I've been fortunate in that I continue to make new friends, and get to maintain strong and precious bonds with my long-term buddies. One thing's for sure, I could never be bored with friends like mine. I see posts on Facebook at times that have rules for friendship and it drives me crazy. You know the ones, 'a true friend does this or doesn't do that' kind of rubbish. Friendships are flexible and organic... different folks for different seasons and reasons. We can have super-close, inner-circle buddies, then those who are still close, but not quite as intimate, and dozens more who are there on the perimeters of life, important and influential, but not quite as close as the others – AND they can be interchangeable. Don't put pressures and rules upon your friendships – just go with the flow and be grateful.

An appreciation for the finer art of op-shopping is one thing me and hubby have in common. Clothes, books, records, unusual hand-made cups and plates, shoes, and almost anything else up for grabs if it has the right price-tag on it (cheap, cheap, cheap). I think we love op-shopping so much because you never know what you're going to get – it's a bit of a lottery. Occasionally I buy something that requires altering and when I do I consult my friend Robin. Robin, a 70-year-old Scottish-dancing, tennis-playing, straight-shooting sweetheart, can sew up a storm. Even with a plentiful supply of tight-fisted Scotty blood coursing through her veins, she's always very generous with her time and expertise. She's also good for a decent hug, a good laugh, a timely cry - and if you're single, male and game enough - a stroll on the beach when the moon is full.

And then there's my buddy Jane, who is as nutty as she is fun, and as generous as she is compassionate. We have a spontaneous friendship where we just 'turn up' on one another. She is one of the very first people to sow (with cold, hard cash) into our dream. Do you know she has done three missions trips in the past 18 months? Recently she served in a voluntary capacity with Joyce Myer Ministries in Uganda, and then she headed-off to Cambodia with them, and as I type this she is serving in Kenya with yet another team. As she 'sows' her time and nursing skills into something far bigger than herself, Jane is finding a sense of purpose and contentment with life that she hadn't known before (there's that 'sowing and reaping' principle in action again).

The loving support of friends helps us to walk fearlessly, to run confidently, and to live victoriously. And because we can be open and honest with one another, when we need to have a decent whinge and whine about our partners in a safe environment we can, and after 'unloading', head back home again to love and embrace them. Just recently I have bonded with a young woman who went to school with my eldest son. Nicole and her hubby are a vibrant young couple with hearts of gold. We have a mutual motivational friendship and a passion for family and the simple things in life. We spur each other on over frothy lattes and gain energy through our connection. Because my world is full to the brim with colourful, stupendous people - both family and friends – I can't help but see the bright side of life. Or, is it because I see the bright side of life that my world is full to the brim with colourful, stupendous people? I'll let you ponder that one.

Round and round the encouragement and love go, people sowing into me and me sowing into people. If you don't have that in your life, start praying for things to change (and, like me, make sure YOU are on the top of the list of things that need changing). Step out and make an effort to create new friendships, and consider rekindling some of the old ones. Don't worry about what's 'normal', or what other people may think or say, just get out there and make some friends (you can see what a rag-tag, eclectic bunch my friends are). There's simply no place for 'lone-ranger' heroes if you want to live a healthy, balanced life. Now I don't mean that we have to live in each other's pockets (heck NO), after all, you may be the quiet, solitary type to 'sing in the wilderness'. But we were all designed to include others into our world. People need people: I need people, you need people, we all need people! (Sounds like great lyrics for a song.)

Hmm, let's take a second here - maybe you already have a network of friends, but they aren't necessarily the type of friends that build you up, encourage you, and bring the best out in you. That's OK, we can work with that. Maybe YOU are the one to make a difference in your circle of friends. Someone has to start the ball rolling in the right direction, and it might as well be you. By drawing on the principles in this book, you can transform your life, and afterwards, you can allow that to permeate your friendships. One of the keys is to remember that there is always 'influence' in a relationship, and it goes both ways. Focus on bringing positive vibes 'to the table' every time you're with your friends, and be aware of any negativity that others bring. The trick is to disarm negativity and criticism before they take control of the situation. You don't need to be a kill-joy, or an overly-pious, pain in the posterior though; just steer the conversation in a positive, uplifting and encouraging direction. Be thankful for what you have, and take every opportunity to express your appreciation for your friends, pointing out their good qualities and their gifts as often as you're able. I've found that people are generally so starved for praise and encouragement that it rarely fails to impact them in a positive sense. But make sure it is genuine and not just flattery, as nobody really appreciates a 'suck-up' or 'butt-kisser'.

Before long you should notice a shift in many of your relationship dynamics. Most people respond to love and encouragement in a positive way, but not everyone. It may seem harsh to say, but some people are so stuck in their misery that you may have to give them a wide berth for a while and consciously limit the time you spend with them, particularly if they're resistant to change. If you chose to take on these recommendations you may even lose some friends, but the friendships you do retain will be far more healthy and mutually-satisfying than they ever were.

The ball's in your court, and you get to choose whether you and your circle of friends will be an influence for good, or a negative influence. Sir James Barrie said, 'Those who bring sunshine to the lives of others cannot keep it from themselves.' There may be some decisions you need to make, and a little more sunshine you need to spread, but your life can and will start to move in the right direction if you want it to.

Don't look at the way your life is and ask WHY, look at the way your life could be and ask WHY NOT?!

CHAPTER TWENTY THREE
dunny ministry

I must be a success, because, according to Facebook, I have 649 friends. I'm not sure who they are or where they're from, or why we've become such good buddies now, but there you have it. I attempt to be faithful to these friends by adding an update to my status or a 'like' against someone else's posting every couple of days. I download pictures of our travels, or a photo of a grandchild doing something cute (*everything* my grandchildren do is cute) straight from my mobile phone and add a 'life message' to it; encouragement and stuff. It isn't the latest iPhone, but Granny's equivalent to it. My eldest daughter is usually the most likely to comment on my photos, and her comments on my 'for-all-the-world-to-see' Facebook profile, are endearing thoughts like, 'Mum, that photo is ridiculously blurry', and 'why don't you put your glasses on Granny' (special mother-daughter moments like those).

I do like my mobile phone though. I had a love affair with it during the first few years, that honeymoon period where I couldn't put it down; I had to be in constant contact with it, and on it all the time. Now the honeymoon is over I give it less attention, but no less love. It is an essential tool in the garden-shed of my life. It is never far from me. I probably only make one or two phone calls a week, and that's on a good week. Even the conversations I do have are usually short and sweet. No, I'm really not much of a 'talker'; I'm more of a 'texter'. Even in today's technologically-advanced communication age, I must say I do still prefer the *written* word. To tell you the truth, I'm quite a rabid texter, pumping out dozens of quirky sayings each week (some of them you will be all too familiar with by the end of this book). It is my preferred way to love on my family and friends, and it is through the many random texts and 'posts' that I let people know I'm thinking of them. My 'love, joy and happy-vibes' thoughts have become sort of a Chrissy trademark over the past six years or so. There's something magical about 'a word in season', as the scriptures put it, where an encouraging word or loving thought arrives on someone's laptop or mobile screen at exactly the right time. It's like a random act of kindness - blessing others because I'm so blessed – and I must say, it gives me a real kick. I love it so much, and have had such positive feedback over the years, that bringing encouragement to at least one person is now one of my daily goals.

My hubby has a saying he's fond of, 'Everything in life involves a trade-off'. What he means is that when we want something, it often means that we have to be prepared to give something up or forgo something, to gain that thing. Life is usually give and take, not take and take. If you're serious then, about reaping certain things in your life, you need to be equally serious about sowing certain other things. There's an exchange of sorts, and you may need to take things up, or lay things down - that's the trade-off. So be it. That's the balance of life. Never fear though, because when we sacrifice anything to fulfil our vision and reach our goals, we invariably gain much more than we lose. So, 'Keep your eye on the prize', as Paul says in the bible. Or as that big, loud-mouthed, cartoon rooster, Foghorn Leghorn used to say, 'Keep your eye on the ball, boy; your eye on the ball.'

And remember, in it all and through it all, *just be you!* I'm sharing bits and pieces of my life to encourage you to live yours more fully, not to copy me or anyone else. By doing your thing, and doing it well, you will encourage others and liberate them to do their thing.

* * *

Prior to taking an invigorating hot shower, enjoying a scrumptious dinner, and re-opening my laptop to sit here and write, I had just returned from a day at The Olive Tree - situated beside the clear, clean waters of the Clyde River, tucked neatly between mountain and sea.. it is officially an art gallery and a café, but as I've shared, it is so much more than that. The Tree is housed in an old heritage-listed building which was the original school, built in 1893, and is becoming quite 'the hub' of the community, with a wide diversity of people and groups coming together regularly to enjoy its friendly ambience and soulful charm.

No matter what mood I'm in as I wake for the day, I make a decision to be happy when I enter the doors of The Tree. I have to sacrifice my self-indulgences, lay any grumpiness down, and be ready to love, accept, embrace, and serve, all those who enter (that doesn't necessarily include my hubby ha-ha). Of course there are days where being friendly and sociable is at the bottom of my wish list, and times where people are decidedly painful to be around, but I'm without excuse. I have a job to do, and my goal is to do it well. For my sake as much for the customers' sake, I try to wear the 'nice' Chrissy wherever possible and try to adopt the attitude that the customer is always right (even though my hubby is quite adamant that, 'the customer is rarely right'). As I've already mentioned, The Tree is an initiative of the local church, and because we are representing the church (and therefore, God), I feel obliged to leave the sour, bossy, self-indulgent, and sometimes impatient Chrissy at home.

So I *choose* to love it. I *choose* to love life. It didn't come easy to me at first as you are well aware, and the reality is that it still doesn't always come easy. I wasn't always an accommodating person, quite the opposite really, but I encouraged myself through my misconceptions, poor self-image, neediness and stuff-ups. I now try to make daily decisions that will allow me to become the woman I want to be. Fortunately, I'm now not the type to give up believing the best of me and the best for me. I've been through enough struggles to understand that nothing worth having comes easily.

I refuse to quit. And why would I? Me and hubby may be only part-way through our dream, with a way to go yet, but we are 'walking' and living in something we used to only think about. We have an outrageous dream to change the world (by encouraging one person at a time – that includes you), and I am so pumped and so thrilled about what comes next that I really want to (and need to) be faithful in what comes NOW (I just made that up - what a great quote for you to add to your quote book). Socrates kept it real: 'Let him that would move the world, first move himself.'

Author and philosopher, Henry David Thoreau says this about dreams, 'If you have built castles in the air, your work need not be lost; that's where they should be. Now put the foundations under them.' For my money, there's no sounder foundation than putting your hopes and dreams in the hands of our Creator. Thoreau goes on to encourage us, 'If one advances confidently in the direction of his dreams, and endeavours to live the life which he has imagined, he will meet with a success unexpected in common hours.'

King David is considered one of the greatest kings of history, and it isn't because he cleaned-up the giant Goliath when he was just a teenage boy (even though that is a ripper story), and it sure isn't because he always did the right thing (because he didn't). David was considered a great king because he was quick to admit his guilt when he had done the wrong thing, and he knew that without God on his side he didn't have a hope of making his life a success. David wrote many of the beautiful, heart-felt psalms in the bible, and he would often cry out with words like, 'My heart longs for you, like a dry and weary land without water'; and, 'Create in me a clean heart, and renew a right spirit within me.' Talk about inspirational writings for your quote book. If you go straight to the bible you could cut-out the middle man. Hang on a minute I *am* the middle man... woops. Of course what I meant to say was, finish reading this book *first*, then move on to the word of God. And if you get into the word of God, the word of God will get into you (one of those old Christian clichés I love to use).

Hey here's some trivia for you: Psalm 119 is the longest Psalm; Psalm 117 is the shortest; Psalm 118 is the centre of the whole bible; and the central scripture in Psalm 118 is verse 8 which says, 'It is better to take refuge in the Lord than to trust in people'. How cool. You know, of all the ancient books and manuscripts ever written - both religious and secular - the bible stands so far above and so far removed from them all in its complexity, authenticity, and sheer mathematical genius, that it's like comparing the 'Encyclopaedia Britannica' to a children's story book. Only a book inspired and written by God himself could claim to reveal the beginning and the end of all things – and everything in between. Even with all his wisdom and understanding, God is still a funny, funny guy. And like any good dad, he loves to PLAY with his kids. I'm convinced that a lot of the stuff in the bible is there just to challenge and stretch our minds, and in many cases, BLOW our minds! It really is an incredible book!

My life-changing meeting with God at the age of 20, when he got my attention at a very crucial time in my life, was through a bible. I mean, I was a goner if he didn't intervene when he did, the way he did, and the only tool he used was his word. I wonder if that's why I'm so passionate about it. I mean, I just love that book. It never ceases to amaze me. My bible (given to me by my good friend Elaine) has been rebound, patched-up with sticky-tape, written all over, highlighted, and has some great sermon notes scribbled in the margins. It's a very *well-used* book. I've read it from cover to cover seven times, and because seven is one of God's special numbers, I reckon that must make me pretty damn super-spiritual don't you? As you can gather, my bible doesn't sit on the shelf collecting dust, but plays a central part in my life. My hope is that you'll allow it to work its way under your skin and into your life.

Like The Tree, the bible is about people from all walks of life with all sorts of gifts and talents (and hang-ups). Pick a version of it that works for you - one that speaks your language. When you get that bible let it speak into your life, your vision, your purpose. In Psalm 119 (yea, the longest Psalm, *so don't* start there) he promises to be a lamp to your feet and a light for your path. God's excited and pumped about showing you the 'right road' for your life, and in the process he'll reveal all sorts of crazy stuff that is guaranteed to blow your mind, and rock your world.

It's been said that people tend to put a lot of emphasis on the particular way that God spoke to them and got their attention. For me, I was saved from suicide by God's word so it's always been special and important to me. I have to tell you about my 'dunny ministry'. One of the things I love to do is leave 'pass-it-on' cards (little cards, similar in size to a business-card, with a bible quote and a cute picture on them) wherever I go... usually in the women's toilet blocks I visit on my travels. After five kids, whenever I see a toilet block, I seize the opportunity to relieve my bladder (and, in case you were wondering, I do try to use the toilet rather than the hand basin). I reckon there's no better place to meet God than on the dunny. I pop these little cards beside the flush-button or just above the toilet roll (or *tissue tape* as one of my granddaughters calls it), or at the hand basin. I'm always hopeful that the right person, at just the right time, grabs a hold of it – not just in their hand, but in their heart. Hearing from God could save someone's life. It saved mine!

They may be in that toilet block to do drugs, or to end their life (or strangely enough, they could even be there to simply relieve their bladder) and they get this word, straight from God. It's good for us to remember that all scripture is Spirit-breathed, and therefore so much more than mere words. Whenever God gets involved you can be sure that *life, power,* and *unlimited potential* are there as well. In Paul's second letter to his friend and co-worker, Timothy, he reminds him that, 'All scripture is inspired by God and is useful to teach us what is true, and to make us realise what is wrong in our lives. It corrects us when we are wrong and teaches us to do what is right. God uses it to prepare and equip his people to do every good work.' God said that when his word goes out, it will always fulfil its intended purpose. And when God makes a statement like that you can bet your left ovary that his word will shake things up a bit… or a lot.

Just as in the days of old, there are countless religions still today with gods made of stone, wood or metal, gods who are, for all intents and purposes lifeless, and therefore powerless to change anything. But the real God is alive and active. He created, and he cares about, every one of his kids. You can see why I get such a kick out of leaving these 'pass-it-on' cards all over the place. In a way I guess it's just another random act of kindness; a nice simple, non-confronting one that anyone can do. I wonder, when I finally get to meet God in heaven, will he say, 'Hey Chrissy, see these precious people of mine over here? They're here with me because of you. I met Natalie in a public toilet in Fremantle; Frank over here under a weather-shelter in a National Park; and Suzie was in a bad way when she found that card you left in the shower block in Coolum.' How cool would that be!

I'm pretty sure he's going to be doing just that for the kind-hearted champion who placed that bible in the motel room for me to find. This is where I give a plug for Gideons International. The Gideons are an outstanding, self-sacrificing interdenominational association of Christian business people and professionals who are dedicated to evangelism and distributing bibles throughout the world, placing them in the highways and byways of life, for those in need. They place bibles in hotels and motels, hospitals and aged-care facilities, domestic violence centres, jails and correctional centres, surgeries and waiting-rooms, and they often distribute New Testaments to students in schools, colleges and universities. AND, because they're so passionate about the word of God and what it can do to change a life, they pay for all their expenses with their own hard-earned money. There are literally thousands of stories similar to mine where a word from God, at just the right time, has saved someone's life.

It is an amazing ministry and I have every respect for these people. I was talking with three Gideon men the other day; I know for sure one was in his 80s, because he told me, and the other two were in their 70s. These men had just been out placing bibles in many different organisations throughout our district, and man, were they excited to be alive. They were full of enthusiasm and couldn't wait to get back out there for more of the same. For me, it highlighted that unchangeable law I keep referring to, 'As a person sows, so shall they reap.' These guys were living proof that God always delivers on his promises, and that any time we step out to help others, something good always comes back our way. Not surprisingly, these three gentlemen looked younger, spritelier, happier, and more content than they had any right to be at their age. Each year Gideons International places millions of bibles throughout the world, in dozens of different languages. Wow, can you imagine the rewards that await these faithful servants. And to think, some beautiful Gideon planted a 'seed' in that lonely motel room I found myself in, all those years ago, and it found 'good soil' in me and grew! Crazy hey. That's what I mean about the word of God - it's full of dynamic life and power! Never underestimate what it can do! Oh, did I mention that my big brother, a one-time, staunch atheist, is a Gideon now too? He's not long returned from Uganda (a trip he paid for with his own money) where he was part of a team of 22 Christians from around the world. That small team distributed 300,000 bibles throughout schools and hospitals and on the streets to men, women and children who had only dreamed of one day owning their own bible. You don't know how much that makes my heart sing.

CHAPTER TWENTY FOUR
stupidman

One night after her bath, our youngest daughter, who was three-years-old at the time, came speeding through the house in nothing but a pair of undies and a towel draped over her shoulders, triumphantly shouting, 'Stupidman! Stupidman!'

This child of ours grew up under the nurture and encouragement of her older siblings, so she really did think she was invincible and could do anything. If the big kids could do it, then she could too. She never stopped to consider the years of groundwork the others put into their achievements, she just saw their many successes and talents and believed they were hers to claim too. So she did. Throughout her time at school she routinely topped her classes… and along the way she learnt guitar, got involved in the drama group, was a member of the Student Representative Council, and was selected in a touring Dance Troupe. She had the opportunity to participate in a Model United Nations Assembly in parliament, and had the coveted honour of being voted Prom Queen at a local youth group formal night. As a young teenager she began writing her own songs and performing them in public. Nothing seemed to faze her, and she appeared to have little or no comprehension of the term 'self-doubt'.

What an attitude! To live with childlike faith without limitations - that precious, priceless hope one often sees in children before the 'grow up and face reality' message does its work, and it's lost. Our little 'Stupidman' has become part of family folklore now, and even after all these years it still leaves us with a smile in our hearts. If you haven't picked it up in my retelling, as bizarre kiddie quirks go, anything that began with the word 'super' was interpreted by her as 'stupid'. Our family never went to the supermarket – we shopped at the 'stupidmarket'.

Now if you want to reap good things for your future, (leaping over those tall buildings) you have to be careful what you plant, and where you plant it. In Mark 4 we read about a farmer who went out to scatter seed across his field. Some of the seed fell on a footpath where it was quickly devoured by the birds. Other seed fell on shallow soil with underlying rock. The seed sprouted quickly enough in the shallow soil, but without a well-developed root system, it soon wilted under the hot sun and died. Other seed fell among thorns that shot up and choked out the tender young plants, so that they couldn't produce any grain. Still other seeds fell on fertile soil (that's YOU... and me), and they sprouted, grew, and produced a crop that was 30, 60 and even 100 times as much as had been planted.

We've bound our hearts to God's heart through salvation. Now it's time to bind our hearts to his plans and purpose for our lives. A deep move of his spirit is upon us – we cannot do 'normal' any longer. We have the secret to life – the secret to happiness – the secret to success. Motivational speaker and author Leo Buscaglia says, 'What we call the secret of happiness is no more a secret than our willingness to choose life.' We will not allow our life and our purpose, to be eaten away, to wilt, or to be choked out. Our hopes are planted in good fertile soil where they sprout, and grow, and blossom, and produce abundant crops. We are not who we were before salvation, before connecting to God. Once we inject faith into our vision, we realise we can NEVER go back to an ordinary life. How can we possibly lead a boring, mundane, visionless existence when God has called us to be *extraordinary!*

'Faith is the confidence that what we hope for will actually happen; it gives us assurance about things we can't see just yet.' Hebrews 11. The New International Version puts it this way, 'Faith is being sure of what we hope for and certain of what we do not see.' Just as seeing and hearing are senses; so faith is a sense - a spiritual sense.

You will find that human limitations are nothing to God. So even if you still think you've got nothing to offer, don't sweat it, God specialises in building something out of nothing. Just look at his track record throughout the bible. All he really requires is our willingness. He has invited us to partner with him in his revolutionary plan to establish his kingdom in a world that is hell-bent (excuse my pun) on self-destruction. Whether we choose to be on his side or not, nothing can stop him fulfilling his plans and purpose. We can continue on our merry way, doing our own thing, and face the consequences later on; or we can accept what God offers us: grace instead of law, truth instead of lies, freedom instead of captivity, acceptance instead of rejection, and real spiritual life instead of spiritual death. Read your bible and get to know this amazing God who loves you, this wonderful God who has poured out his grace upon you and offered you a life full of meaning and purpose.

Can God give you a dream and a vision for your life, and then show you how to fulfil it? Of course he can, no doubt about it. As a matter of fact, I think he's more excited about it than we ever could be. If we commit our way (our life) to God, he promises to give us the desires of our heart. And unlike us, he always keeps his word.

For those who need a completely new beginning, in Isaiah 42:16 he promises, 'I will lead you down a new path, guiding you along an unfamiliar way. I will brighten the darkness before you and smooth out the road ahead of you. Yes, I will indeed do these things, I will not forsake you.' I love that God never gives up on us and always believes the best for us, even though he sees the worst of our behaviour and knows our every thought. That's grace for you, and yes it is pretty amazing.

Dare to live your life with purpose. Take time to dream - while you're awake that is. Be gutsy. Be brave. Apathy is so boring, so lukewarm, so damn unexciting and unattractive. That reminds me of a saying I saw on a t-shirt that Tim, a friend of mine, was wearing. It said, 'The brave may die, but the weak never live at all.' So ask him for directions (that's God, not Tim), for the right path to take, and know that no goal is beyond your reach when you trust him, when you follow where he leads you, and when you persevere. And don't worry about what it may take to fulfil your dream, that's God's business. Know your purpose, dream big, and put those God-given talents of yours to good use.

* * *

I want to remind you of the importance of keeping the big picture in mind. Philanthropist John Ruskin said, 'The highest reward for my toil is not what

I get out of it, but what I become by it.' Next time we face hard and trying times, let's remember that difficulty and challenge are what God uses to shake us from our complacency and slumber, to change us and grow us. God is primarily interested in our character development. So be patient and stay on track. And as you celebrate your successes, do it with a thankful heart. Should you encounter failures (which are inevitable if you're even slightly human), seek God's grace, which is always more than enough to meet our needs, and remember the only true failure is if we quit trying. Good intentions count for nothing - it only counts when we *do something!* If we get knocked down, we get up again. It's just another hurdle to get over, another life-lesson to make us stronger and smarter. We are passionate, purpose-driven people who are living life to the full and inspiring others to do the same!

And before we leave these pages and venture out on our amazingly-unique journeys, understand that we were never meant to retire from life. You might retire from the workforce, but real life has no retirement. Our race starts at birth and doesn't finish until death. We are called to run the race (our particular race) and obtain the prize, as Paul tells us in his New Testament letters. Throughout the latter part of his life, Paul faced some of the most extreme situations and yet he never entertained the idea of retiring or quitting. Paul knew his purpose and was focused on fulfilling it – no matter what. Shortly before he was executed he wrote, 'I have finished the race...and now the prize awaits me.' (2 Timothy 4:7-8) He never retired, he FINISHED!

It's only through Jesus and our relationship with him that we can ever fulfil all we were destined to be. He's coming back just like he said he would, and when he does, he's going to take you and me and anyone else who trusts in him, and we're all going to join in the celebrations at 'the party to end all parties' - the party that never ends - and we'll be given our inheritance: our share of eternal life. That's his promise to anyone who puts their trust in him. In the meantime, let's live our lives to the fullest and help others discover this amazing God of love and grace for themselves.

Thanks for *Falling Up Stairs* with me. I hope you enjoyed reading this book as much as I enjoyed creating it for you. Together we CAN make a difference. Together we CAN change the world - one person at a time, starting with you and me. The bible reminds us, if God is for us, who can be against us? If you're on God's side, never fear, you're on the winning side. Be bold! Be strong! Connect with others – be a team-player. Relax and be yourself, and remember that no one else is qualified to do it better than you are.

Dare to dream – Proverbs 13:12 says, 'A dream fulfilled is a tree of life.' May your tree of life bring you deep peace, contentment and joy, and may it provide shelter and nourishment for those around you. And above all, never forget this simple formula for success - Commit your work to the Lord, and then your plans will succeed. (Proverbs 16:3).

Here's to *love, joy and happy vibes* and to your purpose-filled life of outstanding success!

Fly 'Stupidman', fly!

ACKNOWLEDGEMENTS:

The coming together of my life (and therefore this story) could not have been achieved without the love, support, encouragement and hard yards of many, many people. I couldn't shine without you.

Thank you to those dearest to my heart – the coolest, most incredible hubby in the universe (including the black holes) Step Guinery (my lover, my world); that wild bunch that make up this zany family - Ben Guinery; Garren, Cassia, Ella & Mia Walton; Scott, Kelita & Harper Bourke; Caleb, Tess & Peaches Wilde Guinery; Mace, Jordan, Willow, Chili & Hayz Innes; and those wild surrogates Joel Davies and Heather Gleason; my extraordinary mother Janice Aitken. Lifetime buddies Freda (& Dale) Pierce and Karin (& Wei) Moorhouse; bestest bestie Elaine Rogers; Ray & Wendy Allaway; Peter & Susan Poke; Christine Geradts; Jane Channells; Mel Jia; Leann & Larry Hansen; Kay (& Rod) Grainger; zany Miss Elsie; Brendan & Nicole Gorzalka. Our treasured Southland ever-expanding 'family'; my delightful bookclubbers Kerry, Verna, Jacq, Peter, Kerrie, Gai, Chris, Anthony, Sylvia, Andria, Sue, Margaret, Glen, Leanne and Dzintra. Darlink landlord Lizzy May and Monkey Mick; blood brothers Ray and David, and sisters Linda, Karen and Vicki; Nanna Bottrell who taught me to laugh – even if it is at myself; Mum G, Debbie, Michael, Adam, Amanda, Steven & Cruz. The tireless, ever-blossoming Olive Tree family - Phil & Yvette Taylor, Robin Malcolm, Matty Scott, Erina Jones, Annie Riley, Danny and Leonie Graham, Paul and Rhonda, Louise, Justin Potter, Chloe Gorzalka, Kylie, Tony, Kathie, Wayne, Michael, Stacey, Dave & Mana, Doug, Timmy, Jeff & Mikey, and those 50 artists that keep the place organic. Talented musicians Hamish & Tina Richardson; my dinner pals the Dynamic Diners; Miriam – for years of random loving; Dennis & Warren at Tumbarumba, and Baz & Caz. Rev Kev; Judy Hutchings; huge-hearted Sylvia and my extra-special bubbly singing partner Jodie; Bronwyn Evans, who rekindled a friendship with outstretched arms; Kerrie Bardon; Janet Bell; Ursula & Garry Bennett; Jack & Georgie & their clan; Rosemary & Dean; Pastors David and Jan Youens; Donna & Harrison; Tim, Tarryn & treasures; Terry & Sandra Parkinson; Leanne Todd; my primary school twin Suzanne Thompson; Beetle Bailey; Innes clans; Sammy Turtle; Little Chris. Pastor Sharon Wright; Carrie; Pastors Neil & Ruth Cowling; Karisa; Eagle Nest Alan; Wagga Jim, Sue & Judy; Ray & Margaret Walton; Sarah Warren; Rosie & Griff at Cupitt's Winery; fellow writers Tony & Marisol; farmers Max & Jodie and your brood, Adam, Lisa, Dan & Belinda; Lou; Burg and Purno. Dad, Heidi, Kathy, Peter and Grant – RIP - how I wish you were here to share this. Mechanics Wayne Horsefall and Dan Vagg for keeping Buzz on the road; those cousins who helped me get up to no good and continue to share my life, Maz, Erko, Craig, Kathleen, Nigel, Mark, Philip, Rhonda, Ivan, Peter, Adam, Scott, Johnny, Melda & Fred, Bluey & Zoe, Greg, Michele, Emma & Sarah, Tommy, Robyn, Donna & Robert. Rodrigo; Joel & Jessie and the twins; Lucas; Craig & Richard Walpole; Terry; Bourke buddies Pastor George Mann and the crew and precious little Lynea; Surfbeach landlord Chris; Dave & my 'counsellor' Donna Hunter and Miss Chloe Cundy; fellow travellers Peter and Sue Watt; talented set-your-hand-to-anything Joe Innes; Pastor Scott Hanzy for your exuberant encouragement; inspirational Glenda; Bruce, who has loved me through texts and beyond; Feathered Friends and Nashberries, who allow me to be their weirdest groupie; Inverell friends Marie, Joan & Herbie, Pastors Greg & Lyndall; Maddie & Matty; Jo West-Field; Cheryl Hobson, Allan & Ann McDonald for taking me under your wings; Suzie McGrath for your voice so strong & your men Ian, Chris and Mick; fireside buddies Graeme Jolly, hippies Helen & Peter and James Paull. Brett & Anne McLachlan for unconditional love; Tom & Aimee with your hearts of gold and your rare innocence; Kelly & Rowan Brown; Apo Network Leader Pastor Tim Jack; Jess Fondicaro; Pastors Mark & Liz Youens who trained and released; Pastors Josh & Sarah Geradts, and of course, Jonny boy; huge-hearted Rosemary & Geoff; Times & Express teams; editors extraordinaire Stuart Carless, Lynda Fowkes and the talented, amazing Katrina Condie. Nancy Muldrew, Gary & Sue, Jo & Luis, who housed us when we were homeless; delightful and colourful Celestine, who always believed the book was within me; my ukulele buddies who ensure music remains in my heart; Alex Irvine; one of the many Gideons who set my life in motion; Fogues; Natalie Childs, who provided fitness accountability; accountant Bill Frazer; long-time buddies Carl & Michele and Adrian & Vanessa and Helen; Collette; Robbie in Coolum; Pastors Dave & Kriselle and Rissi; Aunt Denise. The FuS devoted proof-readers Steve, Graeme and Kerry. Photographers Wayne Riley, Matt Scott and Tess Guinery. The incredibly talented team Garry & Michelle at Harbour Publishing House, Daniel Butler and book-sister Penny Brayshaw – I love doing life with you guys! And the rest of you: all of you who love us… those who fed us, housed us, inspired us, financed us, sowed into our dream, provided shelter, clothing & encouragement- we continue because of you. And the many Twitter, Facebook and Instagram daily friends who bring inspiration at the touch of a button. And you.

MORE BOOKS BY CHRISSY GUINERY
Adult:
Room to Breathe

Children's Books:
Meet Mr Mouse, co-written with nine-year-old Willow Innes, illustrated by seven-year-old Chili Innes

Buzz Loves His Friends, illustrated by nine-year-old Mia Walton

Find out more at:
www.chrissyguinery.com

WHAT PEOPLE ARE SAYING

Chrissy's words come from the heart and make me proud to be different. **Nathel**

Chrissy's energetic style takes you on a ride akin to kayaking down river rapids. It's full and fast and then hits an eddy before careening over the waterfall! *Falling Up Stairs* is vibrant, casual and infectiously enthusiastic, but above all its authentic and very engaging. **Karin Moorhouse, author**

Falling Up Stairs is more than a book – it is an event to be thoroughly, absurdly enjoyed – and definitely to be given as gifts for everyone on your Christmas list. You will laugh out loud & you will cry. You will be motivated & inspired and you won't be the same after the journey!
Elaine Rogers, NSW Royal Agricultural Society Events Coordinator

Room To Breathe, amazing, just wonderful! I am inspired!
Judith, Global Care Worker

I was able to give *Falling Up Stairs* to a girl who had just tried to commit suicide. Your decision is life-changing for so many. **Ashleigh**

So true, Chrissy, a touch of zany a day keeps the blues away. **Lisa**

Room To Breathe is yet another incredibly inspiring idea from Chrissy Guinery, like everything she puts her hand to, whether public speaking or writing, she creates connections that help others shine and builds a sense of community and hope into hearts and minds. **Counsellor Donna Hunter**

I have loved, loved, loved *Falling Up Stairs*. I can't wait to have more copies to be able to give out to people. It is such a world-changing book. Tinglingly invigorating in her words. **Ruth**

Chrissy encourages obedience and freedom – at the same time! **Esther**

Reading *Falling Up Stairs* has ignited that fire in my husband's and my soul again.
Monica

Chrissy's words make me think, challenge me and have brought back my smile.
Julie

Chrissy's soul holds a hidden beauty that leaves a sparkle of light on the world.
Kath

Chrissy's words breathe life into me. **Donna**

Buzz Loves His Friends is an excellent resource for linking numeracy and literacy in an approachable and fun way within the classroom.
Lauren Edwards, NSW PrimaryTeacher

Oh, Chrissy has such an inspiring way. Her abundant energy and capacity for love and joy- bubbles never diminishes. **Mary**

Chrissy Guinery helped me recalibrate my life for happiness. She is raw & real, challenging & funny. **Steve**

Chrissy is so inspirational. I thank her for sharing her life, it's amazing!
And *Falling UpStairs* has definitely put thoughts in my head. **CB**

Chrissy is always planting something in someone. I am grateful for her encouragement.
Laughter is a major key for me right now! **Jacquie**

Thanks Chrissy Guinery, for reminding me about the right thing to do. I need a kick up the backside now and again. **Kellie**

Chrissy Guinery changes the atmosphere wherever she goes. **D&D**

What great ideas in *Falling Up Stairs!* Just the thing to enhance self-esteem, individuality & have fun! **Greg**

I am grateful for the way Chrissy shares her journey in *Falling Up Stairs*; some days her words are exactly what I need to hear. She is a blessing to many. **Narelle**

Chrissy's blog Today's Inspiration came just when I needed it. She is a shining light in some of my dark, confusing and lost times. She inspires me and so many others. She is a vessel of God's love and grace. **Julie**

Falling Up Stairs is an easy read. It is fun, inspirational, deep & light-hearted – a book cocktail of delightfulness! Chrissy continuously interacts with the reader in an engaging writing style that makes the reader feel as though we're in a conversation together. It is almost like Chrissy is allowing me to be part of the story, and in so doing, is inspiring me personally to be all that I can be.
Tess, co-founder of The Grey Girls